A SHORT HISTORY

OF IRELAND

J. C. Beckett

Professor of Irish History
in the Queen's University of Belfast

οἰκέομεν δ᾽ ἀπάνευθε πολυκλύστῳ ἐνὶ πόντῳ
ἔσχατοι

HUTCHINSON UNIVERSITY LIBRARY
LONDON

HUTCHINSON & CO (*Publishers*) LTD
3 Fitzroy Square, London W1

London Melbourne Sydney Auckland
Wellington Johannesburg Cape Town
and agencies throughout the world

First published 1952
Second edition 1958
Reprinted 1961, 1964
Third edition 1966
Reprinted 1967, 1968, 1969
Fourth edition 1971

72 - 188414

Printed in Great Britain by litho on smooth wove paper
by Anchor Press, and bound by Wm. Brendon,
both of Tiptree, Essex
ISBN 0 09 109680 4 (cased)
0 09 109681 2 (paper)

A SHORT HISTORY OF IRELAND

History
———

Editor

PROFESSOR JOEL HURSTFIELD
D.LIT.

Astor Professor of English History
in the University of London

CONTENTS

PREFACE TO REVISED EDITION, 1971

In this edition the final chapter, 'Ireland since the Treaty', has been completely rewritten and the narrative brought up to the opening of 1971. Some further additions have also been made to the reading list.

20 April 1971   J.C.B.

PREFACE TO REVISED EDITION, 1966

Though I have made some further changes in the text, and added some recent books to the reading list, this book remains substantially in the form in which it first appeared. In Chapter 6 'Ireland since the Treaty' I have made no attempt to cover in detail the events of the last fifteen years, but I have tried to indicate, very briefly, the character of the changes that have recently taken place in Irish political life.

February 1966   J.C.B.

PREFACE TO REVISED EDITION, 1958

I have taken the opportunity provided by this reprinting to make some minor changes in the text and to re-cast the reading list.

July 1958   J.C.B.

PREFACE TO FIRST EDITION

The task of writing a general history is almost bound to be a thankless one. Selection and compression are its necessary foundations, and both expose the writer to criticism. No two historians will agree on what should be excluded, and it is hard to compress without either obscuring or over-simplifying the issue. To such criticism there is no answer; for no one is more acutely aware than the writer himself how much has been left out and how imperfect is his exposition of what remains. But after all it is idle to blame a small book for not being a big one; as Dr Johnson said, 'All claret would be port if it could.'

Within the narrow space at my disposal I have traced the historical background of the two states of contemporary Ireland. I have no theory to vindicate, no policy to defend. I am concerned only to disentangle a confused stream of events and to make the present situation intelligible by showing how it arose. To this end I have thrown most weight on the modern period, and this has involved some concentration on Anglo-Irish relations. This concentration is not unreasonable, for English influence has been the strongest and most continuous force in the development of our political institutions and our economic life. At the same time, Irish history is not just a department of the history of England. The 'English in Ireland', like the institutions they brought with them, were modified by transplantation, and even when they clung to a connection upon which they believed their political and economic security to depend they continued to regard themselves as Irishmen. For this reason I have refused to define the term 'Irish' in any narrow racial or linguistic sense, and have tried to write a history of the whole country.

The task has been made easier by the great development of Irish historical studies which has taken place during the last fifteen years and which has contributed to a broader and more unified understanding of Ireland's past. Whatever merit this book may possess as a new presentation of Irish history is due very largely to the work of others, but I am particularly indebted to Professor G. O. Sayles of Queen's University, Belfast; Dr R. B. McDowell of Trinity College, Dublin; Mr David Kennedy, MSC; and Dr J. L. McCracken, all of whom read portions of the book in typescript and gave me the advantage of their criticism and advice. Mr J. L. Lord, MA, read the entire work in proof and made many valuable suggestions. My thanks are also due to Sir Maurice Powicke, the editor of the series, for his help and encouragement. It should perhaps be added that I myself am wholly responsible for the opinions expressed in this book and for any errors that it may contain.

Belfast
December 1951

J.C.B.

I

ANCIENT AND MEDIEVAL

I. IRELAND BEFORE THE NORMANS

Irish history, like the history of other countries, has been strongly
influenced by geographical factors. For many centuries Ireland
lay outside the main current of European life, but her insular
position and comparative remoteness gave no lasting protection
against invasion. An island people without command of the sea
was easily open to attack, and Ireland's broad, slow-moving
rivers offered convenient access from the coast to the interior.
But isolation had its effects. Immigrants with their backs to the
sea mingled readily with the preceding population, and the
people of Ireland today are remarkably homogeneous in their
physical characteristics. Though the interior can be reached
easily from the coast, Ireland has no natural focal point, no great
crossing-place of routes, no centre from which influence spreads
naturally to the circumference. This was one of the factors which
helped to prevent the establishment of political unity from within.
Dublin is essentially an invaders' capital; founded originally by
the Norsemen it became the centre of Anglo-Norman power in
Ireland chiefly because of its position on the east coast, within
easy reach of the ports of Bristol and Chester. This brings us to
the most significant factor in the political geography of Ireland,
the position of Great Britain as a barrier between Ireland and the
continent. In historical times almost every important influence
which has reached Ireland from the continent has been filtered
through Great Britain. Today, when English political power has
receded, English influence remains predominant in many spheres

of life. The language of the vast majority of the people is English,
our fashions in clothes and food, most of our magazines, our
newspapers, our fiction, our films, come to us from England;
above all, Ireland remains a country of the common law. This
close and inescapable link between the two islands is the basic
factor in Irish history.

The ancient Gaelic writers carry the history of Ireland as far
back as Noah's flood; modern archaeologists find traces of human
occupation for many thousands of years before Christ; but the
cautious historian has to be content with a more recent beginning.
The Gaels, or Goidels (with whom this beginning can best be
made), probably reached Ireland during the first century B.C.,
coming directly from Gaul. They found Ireland already occupied
by a mixture of peoples, the descendants of earlier invaders from
Great Britain and the continent, and some at least of these peoples
probably spoke a Celtic dialect similar to Gaelic. The Gaels
treated the existing population in much the same way as they
themselves were to be treated by later invaders: they killed some,
dispossessed others and compelled the rest to pay tribute. In
spite of their iron weapons they made a very slow conquest and
the pre-Gaelic population, especially in the north, long retained
its independence. The epic poem *Táin Bó Cualgne* (The cattle-
raid of Cooley) tells how the 'men of Ulster' led by Connor Mac
Nessa and the Red Branch Knights, aided by the heroic Cuchulain
('the hound of Ulster'), defended the north against the 'men of
Ireland', led by Queen Maeve. The details are legendary, but the
general theme represents an historical reality.

Even when the Gaelic conquest was complete, which cannot
have been before the fifth century A.D., the Gaels formed only a
dominant minority, an ascendancy class, holding the best land
and trying to concentrate political power in their own hands.
Though there was a steady mingling of population, the formal
distinction between 'free' and 'tributary' tribes remained until the
twelfth century. But long before this the Gaels had imposed their
language and their legal system upon the whole country, and
Gaelic historians and genealogists had reconstructed the past so
as to obscure the great diversity in the origins of the population.

On the continent the Gaels had been organised in aristocratic
republics, but in Ireland they adopted monarchical government.
To begin with, there was no idea of a united monarchy for the

whole island. Instead, there grew up a vast number of tiny states, each governed by a king or chief elected by the freemen from among the members of a ruling family. The boundaries of these states were ill-defined, for the king's authority was personal rather than territorial. These small states naturally tended to form into groups, each dominated by one relatively powerful ruling family, and this process was aided by the traditional division of the country which the Gaels found on their arrival——the 'five fifths of Ireland'. In fact, it does not appear that this five-fold division ever existed in historical times; but by the fifth century there were seven 'provincial kings', each ruling directly a small state of his own and exercising an external supremacy over a group of other similar states. The political pattern was logically completed by a 'high king' (*árd rí*), himself ruling a province and exercising supremacy over the other provincial kings. But this is a comparatively late development; it was probably not until the fifth century that a claim to such a general superiority was first put forward by the kings of Tara. Even when a high king had secured general recognition by making 'the circuit of Ireland' and exacting hostages from the provincial kings his authority was little more than nominal. The condition of Ireland at this time resembled in some ways that of ancient Greece: there was no effective political unity, but there was a cultural unity based on language, religion and law. Like other Celtic-speaking peoples the Gaels practised a form of Druidism, and this was common to the whole country; but while Ireland remained comparatively isolated, the sharp contrast with the foreigner, which is needed to give such community its full significance, was lacking. In theory, the legal system should have been a more effective bond. It was built up on collections of rights and precedents recorded and interpreted by the 'brehons', a class of professional lawyers, from whom the whole is usually called the 'brehon law'. But this law had no regular sanctions; the brehons were arbitrators rather than judges and their decisions could be enforced only by private action or public opinion.

For many centuries after the Gaelic invasion Ireland remained comparatively isolated. The Romans made no attempt at conquest, and though there was some intercourse with Britain and the continent, the Irish were outside the main stream of European development. When they do appear, at the end of the fourth century and the beginning of the fifth, it is among the barbarians whose savage raids helped to break down the declining Roman civilisation of Britain. In one of these raids a Christian boy of sixteen, a Roman citizen, Patrick by name, was carried off to Ireland as a slave. A few years later he escaped, and after studying in Gaul and being consecrated bishop, he returned to Ireland to preach the Gospel. According to the traditional account, St Patrick landed in County Down in 432 and died in 465, and within that brief period traversed almost the whole country, establishing churches and appointing bishops and priests. Modern scholars query these dates and confine the personal exertions of Patrick to a relatively small area. But the fact remains that before his mission the Christians in Ireland were few and scattered, with no ecclesiastical organisation and no bishop; after it the church was firmly established, and paganism, though still strong, was on the decline. And all this seems to have been accomplished peacefully; early Christian Ireland has no recorded martyrs.

From the beginning, Irish Christianity developed characteristics of its own. Elsewhere, the church was being built up in lands which had once formed part of the Roman empire, where the tradition of territorial divisions was strongly established; the word 'diocese' was itself taken over from the Roman administrative system. But in Ireland territorial divisions were of secondary importance; the unit of government was an amalgamation of kinship groups dominated by a ruling family, and church organisation followed a similar pattern; the country was not cut up into dioceses, but bishops were attached to particular families. Their great number (Patrick is said to have appointed 300 of them) and the nature of their position prevented them from developing the kind of authority wielded by bishops on the continent. The typical religious centre in early Christian Ireland was not an episcopal see, but a monastery. An Irish monastery did not consist of a compact group of stone buildings. It was a little town of wooden huts, laid out in streets and grouped round a small stone church. Here hundreds of monks lived and worked and prayed together under the rule of an abbot, who was usually elected from among the family of the founder. These and other peculiarities of the Irish church were accentuated by the fact that the political condition of Europe during the centuries which followed the downfall of the western empire made regular communication between Ireland and Rome difficult.

Almost at the same time as Patrick and his successors were establishing Christianity in Ireland the Anglo-Saxon invaders were destroying it throughout a great part of Britain. The British church, which had never been strong or adventurous, made little effort to evangelise them, and the work of recovering the lands lost to Christianity was first undertaken by Irish missionaries. One of the earliest and most famous was St Columba of Derry who founded the monastery of Iona in 563, and from there much of southern Scotland and northern England was evangelised during the next hundred years. Other Irish saints carried on the work not only in Britain but on the continent: St Columbanus in Burgundy and Italy, St Kilian in Saxony, St Fiachra and St Fursa in Gaul, St Livinius in the Netherlands. Wherever they went these saints founded monasteries; Lindisfarne, St Gall, Bobbio, are perhaps the most famous links in a chain which stretched from the British Isles to Italy.

These saints and monasteries were noted for educational as well as for religious zeal. In pre-Christian times the professional scholar had had an honoured place in Irish life and this tradition continued. Though St Patrick himself was not a man of great learning, he had brought Ireland into touch with Roman civilisation before it had been almost completely overthrown by the barbarian invasions of the fifth and sixth centuries. Ireland herself escaped these invasions and so was able to act as guardian and transmitter of much that might otherwise have been destroyed. The Irish monastic schools, partly on account of their learning, partly because of their peaceful seclusion, attracted many scholars from abroad. As teachers, as scribes and as commentators Irish monks rendered great service to Europe, and the revival of learning under Charlemagne owes an incalculable debt to their work and inspiration.

During the sixth, seventh and eighth centuries Ireland was free from invasion; but internal warfare continued. The introduction of Christianity helped to strengthen the cultural links between one kingdom and another, but did little to promote political unity. When, after a long respite, Ireland fell victim to the new wave of barbarian attacks from the north, the country was unable to offer united resistance.

In Ireland as elsewhere in western Europe the Norse attacks began with scattered raids for booty, which were followed by permanent settlements and systematic efforts at conquest. By the

middle of the ninth century Norse galleys had passed up the
Bann to Lough Neagh and up the Shannon to the central plain;
Norse city states, the first real cities in Ireland, had been founded
at Dublin, Wexford, Waterford, Cork, Limerick. The struggle
continued with varying fortunes throughout the ninth and tenth
centuries and reached its climax in 1014 in a battle fought at
Clontarf, on the outskirts of Dublin. Here Brian Boru, the *árd rí*,
defeated a Norse alliance, drawn from the Orkneys, the Hebrides
and Man, as well as from the settlements in Ireland, though at
the cost of his own life. 'Brian's battle', as the sagas call it, was
one of the bloodiest of the age; it was a great blow to Norse
power and a final check to any attempt at a Norse conquest of
Ireland.

The magnitude of this victory and the fact that it was won by
an *árd rí* must not be allowed to hide the fact that there was little
unity among the Irish kings, who were often ready to use the
Norse as allies in their wars with one another. Even at Clontarf
the Irish of Leinster fought against Brian because they resented
his attempt to destroy their independence. In England the
Danish invasions had so weakened Northumbria and Mercia
that the way was prepared for national unity under Wessex; but
in Ireland the provincial kingdoms and provincial rivalries
survived. This stands out quite clearly in Brian's own career. In
the 970s he had established himself against various rivals as king
of Cashel, with supremacy over Munster. He was now determined
to secure the high kingship, which for five centuries had been
confined to the *Uí Néill*, the descendants of the famous fourth-
century king, Niall of the Nine Hostages. The high king of the
time, Malachy II, was waging successful war against the Norsemen of Dublin; but Brian did not hesitate to attack him, and
sent the Norse galleys of Limerick up the Shannon to ravage the
lands of Malachy and his allies in Connaught and Meath. In
1002 Malachy was induced to give way and Brian took the high
kingship. The chronicles speak of this as a 'usurpation', and
though Brian did something to justify his act by trying to make
the office effective, and though his proud description of himself
as 'emperor of the Irish' was not entirely an empty boast, he
accomplished little towards turning Ireland into a national
state. Even the army with which he won his great victory was
drawn almost entirely from the south. With his death all the old
internal struggles broke out afresh; Malachy resumed the high

kingship and Brian's successors had to fight to maintain even
the supremacy he had won in Munster.

It is natural to think of the Norse invasions as a period of
destruction and tyranny. But the Norsemen contributed much of
value to the life of the country, for they were traders as well as
robbers. It was they who first established town life in Ireland, and
these towns were centres of peaceful commerce as well as of more
violent undertakings; their ships carried the hides and wool of
Ireland to Britain and Europe and brought back wine and cloth
and slaves. This town life was scarcely affected by Brian's victory
of Clontarf for the Irish army was too weak to take Dublin or
any of the other Norse strongholds. Indeed, the Irish had no
desire either to expel the Norsemen or to occupy their towns, and
though from time to time the settlers were obliged to recognise
the overlordship of some Irish king, they remained as self-
governing communities, known as 'Ostmen' (or 'easterners'). The
Ostmen soon became Christian, and intermarried frequently with
the Irish, but they remained a distinct people; those of Dublin,
for example, had a bishop of their own who was subject to
Canterbury, and not, like the Irish bishops, to Armagh.

This continued independence of the Norse cities was due at
least in part to the break-down of the high kingship. For 150
years after Brian's death it was the prize of contending dynasties
—O'Brien of Munster, Mac Lochlainn of Ulster, O'Connor of
Connaught. Some sort of succession was maintained; but the
kings were, as the chroniclers say, 'kings with opposition',
exercising little authority outside their own provinces except
what they could temporarily enforce by superior strength. This
long-drawn-out struggle was certainly bringing the country
nearer to effective political unity; but the process was a slow one,
and other events at home and abroad were working together to
prevent its reaching a conclusion. The Norman conquest of
England and the reform movement in the Irish church combined
to bring about a new invasion, which Ireland, even after a century
and a half of respite, was in no position to resist.

The Irish church had been greatly weakened by the Norse wars.
The peaceful life of the monasteries had been broken up and
religion and learning had suffered as a result. There had been
some recovery, especially in Munster, under Brian's vigorous
rule; but the remoteness of Ireland, once a protection, was now

a clog on progress. Ireland, 'a kingdom apart by herself', had little share in the intellectual ferment of the twelfth-century renaissance. At the same time the wider contacts being made through the Norse towns revealed to Irish churchmen the full extent of their divergence from the rest of western Christendom. By the middle of the twelfth century some progress had been made towards reform. A territorial diocesan system was established, and the dioceses were grouped in four provinces under the archbishops of Armagh, Dublin, Cashel and Tuam; each of the four archbishops received his *pallium* from the pope, thus formally recognising his dependence upon Rome. About the same time Cistercian monks were introduced, and monasteries in the European style began to replace the old Irish foundations. Much of this reform was due to the efforts of St Malachy; in 1139 he visited Rome on behalf of the Irish bishops; in 1148 he set out on a second visit, but died on the way, at St Bernard's monastery of Clairvaux. Bernard's *Life* of Malachy shows what an unfavourable idea of the Irish church Malachy's account of it had given, and this helps to explain the readiness with which the papacy supported the Anglo-Norman efforts to establish control of Ireland. Irish churchmen were equally ready to welcome such an attempt. In European countries ecclesiastical reforms had generally had the backing of a strong secular authority. There was no such authority in Ireland able and willing to make the new reforms effective against all the vested interests opposed to them. It was therefore not unnatural that the leaders of the Irish church should look outside Ireland for secular support in their work of reconstruction and should be ready to welcome Henry II as an ally. But though the church prepared the way, it was the internal politics of Ireland which provided the opportunity for Norman intervention.

In the struggle for the high kingship Dermot MacMurrough, king of Leinster, had supported the Mac Lochlainn claim. Consequently, when Rory O'Connor of Connaught seized power in 1166 Dermot found his position threatened. He resolved to seek help abroad, and obtained from Henry II permission to enlist allies among the marcher lords of south Wales, a mixed breed of Normans, Flemings and Welsh. Their mail-clad soldiers, their archers, their skill in fortification, were too much for the Irish, and with their help Dermot speedily recovered his kingdom. The most important of these auxiliaries was Richard de

Clare ('Strongbow'), to whom Dermot gave his daughter Eva
in marriage, and with her the promise of succession to the kingdom of Leinster. This promise was of no force in Irish law, but
when in 1171 Dermot died, Strongbow seized and held Leinster,
including the all-important city of Dublin, despite the opposition
of the high king and of the Ostmen.

It was at this point that Henry II himself intervened. He
came with a considerable army, not to conquer Ireland, but to
make sure that his powerful barons did not establish independent
Irish principalities. He asserted his authority over all the lands
that had been occupied, and though Strongbow received a grant
of Leinster, and Hugh de Lacy of Meath, they were to hold their
lands as the king's tenants. The Norse towns, which were of vital
military and economic importance, were not included in the
grants but were retained by the king in his own immediate
control. As for the native Irish rulers, most of them were quite
willing to recognise Henry as their overlord. They were alarmed
at the military strength of the invaders, and hoped that submission to Henry would protect them from attack; besides this,
Henry was known to have the backing of the papacy and he was
welcomed by the clergy, especially by the reformers, who looked
to him for support. A great national synod was held at Cashel,
by Henry's direction, and decreed many reforms, of which the
general effect was to bring the Irish church into line with the
English. Thus, amid the general approval of ecclesiastical and
secular powers, Henry II established the 'lordship of Ireland',
which was to last for almost four centuries, until another Henry
turned it into a kingdom.

2. THE NORMAN CONQUEST AND THE LORDSHIP OF IRELAND

The arrival of Henry II opened a new phase in Anglo-Irish
relations; but it is misleading to regard the events of these years
as consituting an 'English' conquest of Ireland. The invaders
were Norman, Norman-Welsh and Flemish, rather than English,
and their language and traditions were French. Though Henry II
was king of England the Irish rulers submitted to him personally,
not to the English crown. He simply added Ireland to the many
other dominions which he ruled under various titles and by various
rights. The fact that a few years later Henry transferred the lordship of Ireland to his younger son John, at a time when it was by

no means certain that John would succeed to the throne of England, shows that he did not regard the political union between the two islands as indissoluble.

Henry's brief visit to Ireland had been sufficient for his immediate purpose; but many questions remained unsettled, especially that of the constitutional relationship between the lord of Ireland and the Irish kings. None of them had resisted, but many, including the *árd rí* Rory O'Connor, had made no formal submission, and until he at least had recognised Henry's overlordship there could be no hope of establishing political stability. The church was particularly anxious for a settlement, and Laurence O'Toole, archbishop of Dublin, was one of those mainly responsible for bringing about the treaty of Windsor between Henry and Rory in 1175. By this treaty Rory recognised Henry as his overlord and in return was confirmed in his kingdom of Connaught 'as fully and as peacefully as he held it before the lord king entered Ireland' on payment of an annual tribute of hides. Rory's position as *árd rí* was also recognised and he was to be responsible for collecting from the other Irish kings the tribute due to Henry; but his control was not to extend over the territories 'which the lord king has retained in his lordship and in the lordship of his barons'. At the time of the treaty, these territories comprised the former Irish kingdoms of Leinster and Meath, and the Norse cities and kingdoms of Dublin, Wexford and Waterford.

The system of dual government which the treaty of Windsor professed to set up never worked and never could have worked. Rory's high-kingship had been resisted even before the invasion, and now it was little more than an empty claim; he was in no position to exact tribute on Henry's behalf from other Irish kings and there is no evidence that he ever tried to do so. Whatever supremacy or central authority now existed was vested in the lord of Ireland, and Rory O'Connor had no successor as *árd rí*.

This was not the only element of unreality in the treaty. Henry had promised, at least by implication, to respect Irish territories beyond the boundaries of Leinster and Meath; but he found it impossible to restrain the land-hunger of the barons already settled in Ireland and of those who followed within the next few years. He had confirmed Strongbow in possession of Leinster and had granted Meath to Hugh de Lacy. In spite of some local Irish resistance the two earls rapidly developed their territories:

they carved them up into manors, established sub-tenants, built castles, founded abbeys, granted charters to towns and, in general, reproduced the whole framework of feudal society. Their success was infectious, and other men pressed on into Irish territory. To some of them Henry was induced to make grants, despite the treaty of Windsor; but some of them acted independently, and the king had no effective means of controlling them, or of protecting the rights of Irish rulers who had accepted his supremacy. This expansion did not follow any plan. Individual leaders pursued their own interests and established their own claims as best they could. Their successes were due to their courage and energy and to the superior equipment of their forces. Frequently, also, they were aided by divisions among the Irish. In one native kingdom after another disputed successions and rival ambitions opened the way for intervention, and intervention was followed by conquest. It was by playing on such differences that the Normans gradually established themselves in Munster and in Connaught. In the north the Irish showed an unusual degree of unity, and yet it was here that Norman daring won its most spectacular victory. In 1177 John de Courcy, with a band of some 300 followers, invaded the kingdom of Ulidia, overthrew the combined forces of the northern kings, and established his rule from Carlingford Lough to Fair Head. Later tradition speaks of him as 'earl of Ulster', but there is no trace of any royal grant; to his contemporaries he was simply 'Conquestor Ultoniae', holding by the right of his sword. In both titles there was an implicit claim to the whole northern province; but in fact neither de Courcy nor his successors extended their power west of Lough Neagh and the river Bann.

It was by local and independent exploits of this kind that Norman power spread over Ireland during the fifty or sixty years which followed the first invasion. Such a piecemeal conquest was very different from Norman policy in England a century earlier, when the whole country had been systematically and speedily subjugated. But the difference in policy arose from a radical difference in circumstances. William came to a kingdom which had already achieved some degree of unity and which possessed a working administrative system; he found a political and social organisation which could easily be brought into the feudal scheme; and he was prepared to make this kingdom the effective centre of his power. But in Ireland there was no central

government for Henry to take over, and Irish and feudal law
were so far apart as to make amalgamation impossible without
radical changes on one side or the other. It is significant that
whereas William had promised to govern England according to
the laws of Edward the Confessor, Henry did not—indeed could
not—give any corresponding promise in Ireland: the main reason
for his coming, the establishment of Strongbow in Leinster, was
itself a defiance of the Irish law of succession.

Naturally enough the king was not prepared to spend his time
in this poor and remote dominion, directing a conquest from
which he could expect little profit, but it was his absence more
than any other single factor that made the Norman conquest
of Ireland the haphazard affair which it was. Henry's absence
would have mattered less if he had established a strong government in Dublin, the capital of the new lordship. But just as there
was no planned conquest, so there was, at least to begin with, no
planned scheme of central administration. The king was represented in Ireland by a 'justiciar' (as he was in England also during
his absences from that country), but Henry's jealousy of the
magnates made him unwilling to entrust any one of them with
the office for more than a brief period. The transfer of the lordship to John may have been partly intended to improve the
situation, but it had little effect, for John was a boy of ten at the
time, and even after he reached maturity he paid only one brief
visit to Ireland before his accession to the English throne in
1199. The feudal basis on which the conquered territory had been
settled had, however, necessarily carried with it some framework
of government. The tenants-in-chief formed a council upon which
the justiciar could call for advice, though not for assistance in
the day-to-day work of administration, and the collection of
money payments due from them to their overlord involved the
establishment of some sort of exchequer. Besides this, the division
of Leinster, Meath, 'Ulster' and other lands among sub-tenants
meant the setting up of seignorial courts administering feudal
law. But there was no royal justice in Ireland until King John
established a justiciar's court, which later developed into the
court of King's Bench in Ireland. The appointment of an itinerant
judge about the same time marked another step towards repro-
ducing in Ireland the contemporary English judicial system.

In 1210 John came to Ireland again. His main object was to
curb the power of the barons, for Ireland, like the Welsh marches,

threatened to become a centre of baronial resistance to the crown and a refuge for rebellious vassals. He brought with him a considerable army; and though he remained only two months he marched through a great part of the country, from Waterford to Carrickfergus, westwards almost to the Shannon and east again to Dublin, reasserting royal authority throughout the whole area of Norman settlement. Though he did not do all that tradition has ascribed to him in the way of establishing counties, setting up law courts and building castles, he did leave the Dublin government more effective than he found it. Before his departure he compelled the magnates to swear that they would observe in Ireland the laws and customs of England. No doubt this general extension of English law to Ireland was meant to apply, at least in the first instance, only to the Norman settlers, but it involved the whole problem of future relations with the native Irish. If there was to be, in the long run, a real unification of the country, then the English legal system must be universally applied; if, on the other hand, the king's justice was to be confined to his Norman subjects, then the latter would remain a colony, surrounded by an alien and probably hostile population. The problem was not a simple one. Even within the area over which the invaders were generally dominant there remained large districts under the effective control of Irish kings, vassal states rather than integral parts of the lordship. The application to them of English law would involve a complete overthrow of their existing social system. In the areas where English law prevailed it was the steady policy of the barons to treat all men of Irish birth as 'betaghs' (serfs or villeins), so that the term *hibernicus* (Irishman) became the legal equivalent of serf; and in Ireland, as throughout feudal Europe, the serf was excluded from the royal courts. Thus it may be said that where native Irish rule survived there was no means of applying English law, and where English law was applied there was a strong vested interest against extending it to the Irish. Only the completion of the conquest and a determined central government could have beaten down these difficulties and brought about an effective fusion of the races. For a time such a development seemed possible; but when the opportunity passed the effective 'lordship of Ireland' was reduced to a small and struggling colony.

John's example in visiting Ireland was not followed by any

English king until Richard II came over in 1394, and this absenteeism made the maintenance of a strong central government more
difficult. The weakness of feudalism everywhere was that the
force of royal justice depended mainly on the vigour and ability
of the king, and if royal justice was weak the barons were almost
compelled to settle their differences by war. This is what happened from time to time in every country settled by the Normans
—England, southern Italy, Palestine; but in Ireland it became
almost the normal state of affairs. During the thirty years that
followed John's death the great baronial families, the de Lacys,
the Marshals, the Fitzgeralds, the de Burghs, struggled over land
and succession. In the 'war of Meath' and the 'war of Kildare'
they formed alliances and counter-alliances with one another and
with Irish kings, while the justiciars, feebly supported from
England, found it impossible to maintain order. In these wars the
strength of the invaders was steadily drained away, and here may
be found one of the root causes of the failure of the conquest.
But this was not immediately apparent, and in spite of civil strife
the area of Norman influence continued to expand. The de Burghs
and their allies broke into Connaught; the Fitzgeralds (or 'Geraldines') established themselves in Munster and laid the basis
of a power that was to survive until the sixteenth century; in
Ormonde the Butlers founded a dynasty that was to last even
longer.

By the beginning of the fourteenth century, when this expansion had reached its limits, almost two-thirds of the island
had been brought under the control of the Normans. Their
power extended right round the eastern and southern coasts
from Carrickfergus to Cape Clear. Inland it stretched in two
broad bands, westwards to Connaught and south-westwards to
Kerry. But the Irish, though territorially and politically divided,
were still strong. In the north, Irish kings ruled over most of what
is now the province of Ulster, scarcely disturbed by Norman
power. In Connaught, the O'Connors retained a part of their
ancient kingdom. In Thomond, O'Brien held his own against de
Clare. In the more mountainous parts of Leinster and Munster,
and in the wooded and boggy central plain, many Irish kings
still maintained some degree of independent rule over part of
their former dominions.

In spite of civil wars and racial divisions the government of
the lordship became stronger in the latter half of the thirteenth

century. Most of the settled area was divided up into counties, each with its own sheriff and with its shire-court where the itinerant justices administered the common law. As in England, some lands were governed as feudal liberties, in which the direct operation of royal authority was restricted. But the liberties no less than the counties were subject to the common law; and when it became customary to summon 'knights of the shire' to parliament the liberties also were called upon to send representatives. The parliament of 1297, for example, drew its members from nine counties: Connaught, Cork, Dublin, Kerry, Kildare, Limerick, Louth, Tipperary, Waterford; and five liberties: Carlow, Kilkenny, Meath, Ulster, Wexford. These lists give a fair idea of the territory to which the Anglo-Norman pattern of government had been applied at this time. Membership of the medieval Irish parliament was virtually confined to the settlers, its language was French and its legislation was effective only within the occupied area. But in law its authority extended over all Ireland. The independent or semi-independent Irish kings remained outside the system of counties and liberties, but their lands were part of the 'lordship' and it was the justiciar's duty to maintain contact with them. Very often, it is true, the government was at war with one or more of them; but the justiciar had authority to receive them back into the king's peace, and to protect them from damage so long as they remained within it. This authority over the Irish lands was purely external, exercised through the native ruler, and it was sometimes very shadowy, but it provided a link to hold together the Anglo-Norman and Irish elements in the country in some sort of constitutional relationship. In the early years of the fourteenth century the Anglo-Norman element appeared to be getting stronger. Edward I had compelled the magnates to remain at peace with one another, and the general success of his rule was shown by the extent to which he was able to draw men and supplies from Ireland for his Scottish wars. The more effectively the settled area was governed the more likely it was to expand; and at the end of Edward's reign there seemed, superficially at least, no reason why expansion should not continue until all Ireland had been shired, the intermediate authority of the Irish kings abolished, and the whole lordship brought directly under the rule of the common law.

The failure of this prospect has often been attributed to the Scottish invasion of Ireland in 1315. But though the invasion

certainly gave a fatal blow to the authority of the central government, there were already serious weaknesses in the Norman
position, which might, by themselves, have brought the lordship to virtual ruin. Above all, the number of settlers was too
small. The first wave of conquest had been followed by a fairly
steady stream of knights and barons, but there was no solid
body of English or Anglo-Norman middle-class population.
English and French merchants were established in some of the
towns, notably in Dublin, and William Marshall settled small
free-holders of English birth in parts of Leinster, but generally
speaking, even in the areas most firmly held by the Normans, the
bulk of the people were Irish. In the more remote areas of Connaught and Ulster the Norman veneer was very thin indeed.
Almost inevitably, these isolated settlers began to adopt some of
the habits, and even the language, of their neighbours; before the
end of the thirteenth century the Irish parliament found it necessary to pass laws against 'degenerate' Englishmen,[1] who 'attire
themselves in Irish garments and having their heads half-shaven
grow and extend the hairs from the back of the head . . . con-
forming themselves to the Irish as well in garb as in countenance'.
But the process could not be arrested by statute, and as time went
on many of the settlers conformed more and more to the Irish
way of life. This basic weakness in the Norman position gave the
Irish an opportunity for recovery. At no time during the middle
ages was there anything like a united, much less a 'national',
resistance to the conquest. But individual Irish rulers, though
fighting for their own interests and though generally ready to
recognise the overlordship of the king of England, did set limits
to Norman expansion. After the middle of the thirteenth century
their military inferiority was partly remedied by the importation
of mercenary troops from the Hebrides. These 'gallowglasses'
(*gall-óglaigh*: foreign soldiers) were of mixed Gaelic and Norse
descent and their standard weapon was the great Scandinavian
axe. Unlike the native Irish they wore body-armour, and they
fought with a skill and determination that made them the backbone of every Irish army from the thirteenth century to the
sixteenth. This Irish recovery had not achieved any decisive success
before the Scottish invasion, but it was an important factor in the
situation; for the continued resistance of the Irish, especially in
the north, encouraged the Bruces to make the venture.

1. For the description of the colonists as 'English' see below, p. 31.

The hero of the invasion was Edward Bruce, brother of King Robert. In May 1315 he landed on the Antrim coast with 6,000 Scottish troops and a year later he was crowned 'king of Ireland' at Dundalk. But the title meant little. Despite the high-sounding terms in which Donal O'Neill, 'king of Ulster and by hereditary right true heir to the whole of Ireland', professed to transfer his claims to Bruce, there was in fact no unity and no stability among the Irish. Some joined the Scots, more took advantage of the general disorder to engage in local war against their Norman enemies; but, though Bruce won victory after victory, there was no sign of that national resistance which in Scotland had finally established the unity and independence of the kingdom against the foreigner. At length, in October 1318, excommunicated by the pope, ill-supported or deserted by his Irish allies and with his own forces depleted, he was overthrown and killed at Faughart, not far from the scene of his coronation. It is significant that the native Irish annalists, in recording the events of these years, are chiefly impressed by the ferocity with which the war was conducted and the misery that it produced. To them Bruce is not the champion of Irish independence, but a usurper at whose death they rejoice: 'Edward Bruce, the destroyer of all Ireland in general, both foreigner and Gael, was slain by the foreigners of Ireland, through the power of battle and bravery, at Dundalk . . . and no better deed for the men of all Ireland was performed since the beginning of the world.'

3. THE LATER MIDDLE AGES

The fatal effects of the Scottish invasion upon the government of the lordship were not at once fully apparent. Bruce had failed to win the united support of the native Irish, he had not established a firm hold on any part of the country, and his death was followed by the complete abandonment of his enterprise. For a time it seemed as if the central government might recover the authority it had lost. Donal O'Neill was driven back to the interior of Ulster, other Irish rulers were forced to make peace and the few discontented Anglo-Norman nobles who had supported Bruce returned to their allegiance. But the shock to administration had been too great to admit of any permanent recovery. Disorder and plunder had drained the resources of the country, and bad harvests had added to the general distress. The whole basis of

the settlement had been shaken, weaknesses were made more
dangerous and disruptive forces given freer play.

The most immediate threat was that from the native Irish.
Since the first arrival of the Normans the struggle between the
races had been almost continuous, but throughout the thirteenth
century the general result of the fighting had been the extension
of the occupied area; and though by the beginning of the fourteenth the Norman advance was being generally held in check,
yet even in the midst of the Bruce wars the Irish of Connaught
suffered their heaviest defeat. At Athenry, in 1316, the de Burghs
and their allies destroyed a great Irish army and re-established
their supremacy in the west; henceforth the O'Connor 'kingdom
of Connaught' was reduced to a fraction of its former size and its
ruler became little more than a dependant of the de Burghs. But
this was the last important expansion of the conquest, and it proved
a temporary one. Though the Irish would not unite, they were ready
to take advantage of the disorder produced by the Scottish invasion
to engage in local wars for the recovery of occupied lands. Their
efforts were not consistently maintained nor universally successful,
but they showed that the tide had turned. The thinness of the
settlement and the practice of leaving enclaves of native territory
in the settled areas now began to produce their effects.

While it suffered from these external attacks Norman power
was also being weakened from within. The population of the
settlement was declining. The towns suffered severely from the
Black Death in 1349 and 1350, and there was a steady drift back
to England, resulting from the poverty and insecurity of the
country. This evil of 'absenteeism' had already drawn the anxious
attention of the king, and in various forms plagued Ireland for
centuries to come. It began with the greater barons, who had
lands and interests in England or on the continent as well as in
Ireland and who were often inclined to neglect their Irish responsibilities. Thus, garrisons were allowed to decay, and the sub-
tenants were left to defend themselves as best they could against
the Irish, or to come to terms with them. In such circumstances
they were unlikely to have much respect for their nominal lords
in England or for a government which did so little to protect
them. The dangers of the situation were obvious, and as early as
1297 a law was enacted to compel absentees to make due provision for the protection of their lands. But no penalties were
sufficient to enforce such legislation, and the frequency with

which the government returned to the task is itself evidence of failure. As the Irish revival spread and strengthened, the pressure upon the remaining settlers increased; and now it was the whole body and not just the magnates who were affected. In 1361 Edward III complained of 'the magnates of our land of England', who, having estates in Ireland, 'take the profits thereof, but do not defend them'; in 1421 it was the 'artificers and labourers' who were so 'burdened with divers intolerable charges and wars' that they were flocking daily from Ireland to England. The development was ominous for the future of the settlement.

Amid these dangers, civil strife among the great Norman families tended to increase rather than to diminish. Its result was often to weaken the links which bound them to the crown and to leave their lands open to Irish reconquest. One example must suffice, but it amply illustrates the essential weakness of the lordship at this period. The great family of de Burgh had not only established its supremacy over Connaught but had also succeeded to the earldom of Ulster, where Richard (the 'Red Earl') had done something to remedy, for a time at least, the ill-effects of the Bruce invasion. But his grandson William (the 'Brown Earl') quarrelled bitterly with his own cousins and in 1333 he was murdered at Carrickfergus at their instigation. This might have mattered little had there been a son to succeed, but William's sole heiress was an infant daughter, who was carried off to England by her mother, and almost immediately the great de Burgh inheritance began to break up. In the north, most of the lands that had once comprised the 'earldom of Ulster' fell to O'Neill and O'Doherty. In Connaught the development was different, but no less disastrous for royal authority. Here two brothers of the younger branch of the de Burghs defied the feudal law of succession and divided the family lands between them. Their surname had already been Gaelicised into 'Burke' and they now took the additional name 'MacWilliam', from their father William 'Liath' ('the Grey'). Speaking the Irish language, following Irish customs and intermarrying with Irish families, they themselves virtually became Irish chieftains and lost almost all remnants of their feudal character. Elizabeth de Burgh, the legitimate heiress to Ulster and Connaught, was eventually married to Lionel, son of Edward III. His efforts to enforce his rights were fruitless; but through this marriage the claim passed into the English royal family, to be revived later on by the Tudors.

As the fourteenth century progressed it became more and more evident that there was little prospect of completing the conquest and turning the lordship of Ireland into an effective feudal state embracing the whole country. Instead, the government was forced to concentrate on maintaining rather than on extending the settled area. This policy involved implicit recognition of the fact that the lordship was in reality a foreign colony in the midst of a hostile population, to be kept in existence only by constant border warfare. There was no formal abatement of the full claims of the English crown in Ireland, but in the later middle ages the contrast between those claims and the crown's actual authority, a contrast which had always existed, became much more strongly marked. It appears particularly in the shrinking of the area over which the Dublin government functioned regularly; before the end of the fourteenth century this 'English land' or 'land of peace' was confined to about one-third of the whole country, for by this time most of Ulster and Connaught and much of Munster had passed beyond effective control. But the contrast is also to be seen in a changed attitude to the native Irish. So long as there was a prospect of completing the conquest it was natural to look forward to the assimilation of the races and so to consider favourably the general extension of English law to the native population. Edward I, who was to have experience of the same kind of problem in Wales, had made an unsuccessful attempt to carry out such an extension in the 1270s. Even after the Bruce invasion, another effort was made by Edward III; but though many individuals and families were separately admitted to the privilege of English law it was now too late for a policy of general assimilation to succeed. The Irish were on the attack, the security of the settlement was threatened, and the almost inevitable result was a defensive 'colonial' policy, which finds its fullest expression in the famous 'statutes of Kilkenny'.

These statutes were passed in a parliament which met at Kilkenny in 1366 before Lionel, duke of Clarence, lieutenant in Ireland of his father King Edward III. They included measures for the better defence of the marches against the Irish enemy, for the prohibition of private warfare and for the regulation of trade. But by far the most important were those which aimed at setting a permanent barrier between the two races in Ireland, for it was recognised that wherever they mingled it was the Gaelic influence which predominated. So alliance between them by marriage or concubinage or by fostering of children was forbidden; neither the English (i.e. the Anglo-Norman settlers) nor 'the Irish living amongst the English' were to use the Irish language; the English were not to use Irish names, Irish dress, Irish law, nor to ride without saddles after the fashion of the Irish. Existing laws which excluded Irishmen from cathedral chapters, ecclesiastical benefices and religious houses amongst the English were re-enacted. The statutes of Kilkenny have often been represented as a kind of aggressive 'outlawing' of the Irish; in fact, they were essentially defensive, directed towards preserving royal authority and English influence in what still remained intact of the lordship. To give them greater force, the three archbishops and five bishops present at the parliament published sentence of excommunication against all who should contravene them.

The Kilkenny policy, though supported by these spiritual sanctions and fortified by later enactments, could not be fully carried out. In the church, it is true, the segregation of English and Irish clergy, which was of long standing, was fairly consistently maintained. The distinction was heightened by the fact that in areas where the native clergy were still in control the reforms of the twelfth century had in some respects left little permanent mark on the life of the church. There was no strictly parochial system; bishoprics and religious houses continued to be associated with particular families; even the practice of hereditary succession in ecclesiastical benefices had not disappeared. The dioceses which were 'among the English' were certainly not free from abuses, but in general they stood for a more orderly system of administration. This contrast strengthened the alliance between crown and papacy, and together they managed to exclude the native Irish from the most important posts in the 'English' area. The bishops, abbots and other clergy who attended parliaments or councils were almost without exception of English birth or descent, and their attitude towards their Irish fellow-churchmen seems to have been dictated entirely by considerations of political interest and racial antipathy.

But the segregation which had been established and maintained in the church was impossible in secular life, and the mingling of the races could not be prevented. In Connaught and in the earl-

dom of Ulster the process had already gone too far for any
change to be attempted. The 'degenerate English', as they came
to be called, were not likely to change their long-established
habits at the bidding of parliament. Even in Munster and
Leinster, where royal authority was still of some force, the
Geraldines and Butlers and other leading families were too well
aware of the benefits they derived from their intimate contacts
with the Irish to give them up. Throughout the later fourteenth
century and the whole of the fifteenth, as the real authority of
the Dublin government receded, Irish language, Irish law and
Irish dress became more and more dominant, even in the districts
which had once been most thoroughly settled. In the more remote
areas the settlers became, as the old saying has it, 'more Irish
than the Irish themselves'.

   It must not be supposed that in this mingling of races the
influence was all on one side and that the Irish remained completely unaffected. Irish rulers copied the Anglo-Normans in
various ways. They adopted crests and coats of arms, they used
seals, issued charters, entered into indentures and made written
treaties. These changes, though not unimportant in themselves,
were only symbols of something much deeper, which touched the
core of the Gaelic political system. The main weakness of that
system was the absence of direct hereditary succession by primogeniture; instead, when a ruler died a successor was elected from
among the members of his family. An attempt to secure continuity
was often made by electing a 'tanist', or prospective successor,
in the lifetime of a reigning king or chief, but this was a clumsy
and sometimes a dangerous procedure. Besides, natural dynastic
ambition made many an Irish ruler anxious to establish a family
power by direct succession, and the superior advantages of a
political system based on the hereditary holding of land were very
attractive. These factors working together led to a partial feudal-
isation of the Gaelic political system, which appeared particularly
in the increased personal power of the chiefs, supported by the
employment of gallowglasses under the chief's personal command. These developments did not take place without protest and
resistance. In particular, all attempts to establish hereditary
succession by primogeniture as a fixed rule were unavailing; but
they were not abandoned, and dynastic ambitions and rivalries go
far to account for the succession-wars which tore almost every
part of the country in the fifteenth century, and for the readiness

with which Irish rulers accepted feudal grants of their lands from
Henry VIII in the sixteenth.

The decline of royal authority after the Bruce wars had shown
itself not only in a growing inability to resist Irish attacks, but
also in the weakening of the links which bound the settlers to
England. In one sense these links had never been strong. The
statutes of Kilkenny are prefaced by a declaration that 'at the
conquest of the land of Ireland and for a long time after, the
English of the said land used the English language'. But in reality,
the twelfth-century conquerors were Normans and spoke French,
the language, indeed, in which the statutes of Kilkenny are
themselves written. Just as the Normans in England gradually
abandoned the use of French and took to English, the Normans
in Ireland, or a considerable proportion of them, as naturally
took to Irish. In the trading towns, of course, and in the districts
around them, and among the more important families, whose
contacts with England were fairly close, English came to be
spoken. But even before the end of the thirteenth century, and
without any suggestion of a linguistic test, we find the settlers in
general referred to as 'Englishmen'. They were, however, English
with a difference, and the distinction between 'English born in
Ireland' and 'English born in England' remained a constantly
recurring theme at least down to the eighteenth century. The
statutes of Kilkenny tried to obliterate the distinction, but in
vain, for it represented a real diversity of outlook and interest.

The 'English born in Ireland' (or, as we may now begin to
call them, the Anglo-Irish[1]), though they might profess formal
loyalty to the crown, were not always ready to support its authority.
From the beginning of the conquest the magnates had aimed at
building up family supremacies, usually fortified by alliances with
Irish chiefs—a policy which the statutes of Kilkenny had been
unable to check. They did not, of course, ignore the machinery
of royal government, but when opportunity offered they were
always ready to control it in their own interests rather than in
those of the crown. Thus the crown was almost compelled to
rely for the maintenance of its authority upon Englishmen born,
and the policy of appointing them to the most important posts in
the Irish administration was followed fairly consistently from the
foundation of the lordship. English kings were not prepared to

1. The term 'Anglo-Irish' (here used for convenience) does not seem to have
gained general currency until the eighteenth century.

visit Ireland regularly, nor to devote to the completion of the
conquest supplies of men and money comparable to those which
they poured out on their Welsh, Scottish and French wars, but
they were at least anxious that within the area controlled by the
Dublin government the royal authority should be respected.
Thus, the Irish law courts were subordinate to the English;
English legislation was applied to Ireland, sometimes with the
additional sanction of the Irish parliament but sometimes also
without it; the Irish treasurer was called on to account to the
English exchequer, and other officials of the Irish government
might be obliged to defend themselves in English courts. Down to
the latter part of the fifteenth century these means were sufficient
to prevent the domination of the Dublin administration by an
Anglo-Irish magnate.

But though the crown could keep fairly consistent control of
the government of the lordship, it could not prevent that government from becoming steadily weaker. On all sides the Irish were
pushing once more into the territory they had lost. In the north
Niall More O'Neill had made himself virtually king of Ulster,
destroying all but a few remnants of the Norman earldom; he
even extended his authority into Connaught, where royal authority
was now little more than a name. In Munster the O'Kennedys,
once the subordinate allies of the earls of Ormonde, seized and
held territories which the Butlers could no longer defend; and
both in Munster and in Meath other Irish clans were making
similar conquests. The Irish revival in Leinster was even more
dangerous. In the mountainous region to the south of Dublin
Art MacMurrough Kavanagh, claimant to the old Irish kingdom
of Leinster, was steadily enlarging his territories and stretching
out into the fertile lowlands to east and west, thus building up a
strong Gaelic state within striking distance of the capital. But
this Irish expansion reflected the personal ambition of the chiefs
rather than any 'national' movement. Richard II received personal
homage from both Niall More O'Neill and Art MacMurrough
when visiting Ireland in 1394, and the latter was knighted by
the king's hand. It is significant also that Art MacMurrough
sought alliance of the earl of Kildare and strengthened it by
marrying the earl's sister, despite the statutes of Kilkenny.

The weakening of Anglo-Irish loyalty and the growth of native
power combined to restrict the authority of the Dublin government more and more to a narrow strip of territory on the east

coast. Richard II, during his visit to Ireland in 1394–5, proposed
to recognise this fact, to strengthen a definitely 'English land'
between Dundalk and Waterford and use it as a base from which
royal authority might be re-established over at least part of the
rest of the country. Richard himself had not the resources to put
this policy into execution and his Lancastrian successors were
too busily employed in foreign and domestic wars to attempt it.
By the middle of the fifteenth century the 'English land', or
'English Pale', as it came to be called, had shrunk to much
narrower limits than those which Richard had planned; and so
far from being a base for the recovery of the rest of the country it
lived almost in a state of siege, obliged sometimes to buy off the
Irish on its borders by the payment of 'black rents'. It would,
however, be misleading to suppose that beyond the Pale the
force of royal authority had completely disappeared; over a
fairly wide area it was still formally recognised and sometimes
actually asserted. Eleven counties, of which Limerick was the
most remote, contributed to the parliamentary subsidies of 1421;
parliamentary writs continued to be sent to the sheriffs of Ulster
and Connaught; parliament itself occasionally met in towns far
outside the Pale—in Wexford in 1463, in Limerick twenty years
later. Thus, even at its lowest ebb, the Dublin government
never abandoned the claim to the lordship of Ireland. More than
this, it maintained a bridgehead. The ports of Dublin, Drogheda,
Dundalk and Waterford were open to English shipping and
offered ready inlets to any English king who was prepared to
send forces to reassert his power in Ireland. The way was open,
both legally and physically, for reconquest; but the significance
of this did not become clear until the sixteenth century.

During most of the fifteenth century, while England was being
drained by the disastrous campaigns in France and torn by civil
strife, Ireland was left to go pretty much its own way. The Anglo-
Irish were to some extent affected by the wars of the Roses, which
for them, however, proved little more than a new phase of an old
struggle between Geraldines and Butlers. The former, supported
by most of the Anglo-Irish nobles, were Yorkists, the latter
Lancastrians. The popularity of the Yorkist cause arose at least
in part from the great reputation achieved by Richard of York
as lord lieutenant between 1447 and 1460. He had no genuine
interest in Ireland, but there were both Irish and Anglo-Irish

B

strains in his ancestry; and, more than this, in an effort to mani-
pulate the politics of the Pale to the advantage of his own party,
he supported a claim to legislative and judicial independence put
forward in the Irish parliament. Despite this alliance, the Yorkist
triumph with the accession of Edward IV in 1461 made no
important change in Anglo-Irish relationships. The really significant development of the next two decades was the rise of the
Leinster Geraldines under the earls of Kildare. The way to power
lay open, for after Thomas, seventh earl of Desmond, had been
attainted and executed at Drogheda in 1468 the Munster Geraldines withdrew from the politics of the Pale, and the influence of
the pro-Lancastrian Butlers was in decline under a Yorkist
monarchy.

The Kildare influence had been steadily increasing for over a
century, but it was not until the 1470s that it became dominant.
The seventh earl was deputy[1] at the time of his death in 1477.
The council, which was controlled by the Kildare party, immediately elected his son, Gerald (or Garret), the 'Great Earl'
('Garret More' to the Irish), as justiciar to carry on the government until the king should make a new appointment. Edward IV
attempted to curtail this rising power by sending over an English
deputy, Lord Grey, instead of confirming Kildare in office, as the
Anglo-Irish had expected. But Edward's attempt failed. Kildare
refused to recognise Grey, the chancellor refused to hand over
the great seal, the constable of Dublin Castle refused to surrender
his command, and in the end the king had to give in. Kildare
paid a visit to England and he accepted various conditions, but
he came back as deputy, and the family power of the Kildares,
thus established even against the king himself, dominated Irish
politics for two generations.

The source of this family power was three-fold. In the first
place it arose from Kildare's position as a territorial magnate,
whose earldom, stretching over the modern counties of Kildare
and Carlow and lying partly inside and partly outside the Pale,
enabled him to exercise an almost irresistible influence on the
Dublin government. Secondly, the Great Earl extended the policy
of building up alliances among the native Irish, fortified by
political marriages. It was the power derived from these two

1. The deputy took the place of the lord lieutenant, at this period usually an
absentee, to whom the government of Ireland was nominally entrusted; but the
deputy was directly responsible to the king.

Later Medieval Ireland

Showing area of the Pale and distribution of some of the most important Irish and Anglo-Irish families

sources that enabled him to make effective use of the third, his
control of the deputyship. By itself, this conferred little independent authority, but Kildare was strong enough to use it for
his own ends. Council and parliament gave legal sanction to his
actions; the military resources of the Pale became virtually part
of his private army; the royal revenue was almost as freely at his
disposal as the revenue of his own estates.

The accession of the Tudors to the English throne made little
immediate difference in Ireland. Henry VII followed, of necessity,
a waiting and defensive policy and despite Kildare's known
adhesion to the Yorkist cause he was allowed to remain deputy.
Even after he had openly challenged Henry's authority by crown-
ing Lambert Simnel as 'Edward VI' in Christ Church cathedral,
Dublin, he was continued in office. A few years later the more
serious threat from the intrigues centring on Perkin Warbeck
forced Henry to stronger action, and for a brief period he tried
the experiment of ruling Ireland through an English deputy,
backed by an English army. The deputy was Sir Edward Poynings,
a capable soldier, who succeeded in foiling Warbeck's attempted
invasion in 1495. But the expense of this system of government
was heavy and it soon became clear that the Irish revenue could
not be increased sufficiently to meet it. Besides this, the most
urgent danger from Warbeck quickly shifted to the Anglo-
Scottish border, where James IV was preparing to assist him by
force of arms. So Poynings and the English troops were recalled,
and after a brief interval Kildare was restored.

Poynings' administration left one enduring memorial in the
famous statute which bears his name, 'Poynings' law', which
remained in force, with various modifications, until the legislative
union of 1800, was enacted in a parliament at Drogheda in 1494.
In its original form it laid down that no parliament was to meet
in Ireland until the chief governor and council had first informed
the king and council in England of the reasons why a parliament
was necessary and of the bills to be proposed to it, and had
received licence under the great seal of England to proceed. In
later years this law came to be the great clog on the initiative of
the Irish parliament. But fifteenth-century parliaments, English
or Irish, rarely took the initiative in legislation, and the law was
intended to curb over-powerful deputies; by the peaceful citizens
of the Pale it was looked upon as a protective and not an
oppressive measure.

The restoration of Kildare in 1496 was a clear indication that Henry's policy in Ireland was strictly defensive. He wanted to secure the quiet government of the country as cheaply as possible, and in this he succeeded. Warbeck's last attempt at invasion was driven off in 1497; and for over twenty years, in spite of the increasing naval power and national rivalries of the European states, none of them attempted to weaken the English king by intrigues with his Anglo-Irish subjects. The Great Earl ruled continuously until his death in 1513, extending his influence, through his estates and his alliances, over the greater part of the country and defeating every combination of his enemies, but maintaining at the same time an unshaken loyalty to the English crown. When he died his son 'Garret Oge' (Young Gerald) succeeded almost as naturally to the deputyship as to the earldom. But this peaceful succession marked the beginning of a new and dangerous era, for English policy towards Ireland was changing in a way which would soon leave no room for the feudal independence of the house of Kildare.

2

THE TUDOR CONQUEST

I. THE FALL OF THE HOUSE OF KILDARE

The succession of the ninth earl of Kildare almost coincided
with the advent of Wolsey to power in England, and it was under
Wolsey's influence that Henry VIII first turned his attention to
Irish politics. Though the Kildares had maintained the framework of royal authority and had prevented Ireland from becoming
a centre of anti-English intrigue, the situation in general could
hardly be considered satisfactory. The government of the Pale
was carried on in the king's name, but it was really in the hands
of Kildare and his Anglo-Irish dependants. The Pale itself was
still confined within its old narrow frontiers, and even Kildare
could not always defend it against incursions by hostile Irish.
Beyond the Pale Ireland presented a political patchwork which an
English writer of the period has described as follows:

'There be more than sixty countries, called regions, in Ireland,
inhabited with the king's Irish enemies . . . where reigneth more than
sixty captains . . . that liveth by the sword and obeyeth to no other
temporal person, but only to himself that is strong: and every of the
said captains maketh war and peace for himself, and holdeth by the
sword, and hath imperial jurisdiction within his room, and obeyeth
to no other person, English or Irish, except only to such persons as
may subdue him by the sword. . . . Also, there is more than thirty
great captains of the English noble folk, that followeth the same Irish
order . . . and every of them maketh war and peace for himself, without any licence of the king, or of any other temporal person, save of
him that is strongest, and of such as may subdue them by the sword.'

The boundaries of these 'regions' or petty states (*tuatha* in Irish) were constantly fluctuating; there were conflicting claims to supremacy in this or that area; alliances and counter-alliances were constantly in course of formation or disintegration; and local warfare, which sometimes spread until it embraced almost the whole island, was endemic.

Powerful as the Great Earl had been, it was beyond his strength, perhaps beyond his desire, to impose order on this chaos. He had been satisfied to retain the deputyship and use its prestige and authority to strengthen his own family. His son was to discover that this policy could not long survive active royal intervention from England.

To begin with, Henry attempted no more than some sort of closer supervision over Kildare's government. In 1515 the earl was induced to visit England, but returned with power un-diminished. Wolsey, however, was busy collecting information about Ireland, and four years later Kildare was summoned over again to answer complaints about his administration. This time a full-scale inquiry was launched, and though a charge of treason brought against him had to be dropped he was, in January 1520, removed from the government and an entirely new policy for Ireland was embarked upon. Private war was to be suppressed; Wolsey's legatine authority was to be enforced and the ecclesiastical administration reformed; a parliament was to be summoned and a subsidy collected from all Ireland. The man chosen to carry out this policy was Thomas Howard, earl of Surrey, who was to hold rank not as lord deputy but as lord lieutenant, the first resident lieutenant since the mid-fifteenth century. Surrey was a capable soldier, a great nobleman and lord admiral of England; thus he might hope to outshine Kildare and attract the respect and loyalty which had been refused to a civil servant like Poynings.

The experiment was not a success. Surrey reached Dublin in May and immediately found himself in difficulties. The Irish exchequer was nearly empty, and the £4,000 which he had brought with him was soon exhausted. Almost immediately after his arrival O'Neill invaded the Pale from the north, and though a brief campaign produced temporary peace the situation remained precarious. In the late summer plague broke out in the Pale, and food prices shot up to famine level. By November Surrey was almost at his wit's end—'I and the treasurer with all the captains

of the king's retinues here have not amongst us all £20 in money'.
Some relief from England and some increase in the Irish revenue
enabled him to carry on for a time. But Henry warned him not
to expect continued heavy payments out of the English treasury
and urged him to reduce Ireland by diplomacy, to proceed 'by
sober ways, politic drifts and amiable persuasions'. Surrey was
in a better position than his master to judge the realities of the
situation. At the end of his first year he sent the king a report
arguing that Ireland could be reduced only by force and pointing
out the implications of such a policy in men and money. When
Henry refused to face these implications Surrey asked to be
recalled: 'I have continued here one year and a half, to your
grace's great charges and to mine undoing, for I have spent all
that I might make'. A few months later he was allowed to lay
down his office.

Surrey's brief viceroyalty, though it accomplished little,
revealed two important facts. First, direct government of this
sort was expensive: between April 1520 and March 1522 more
than £18,000 of English money was sent over to Ireland, and there
was no early prospect that the Irish revenue could be increased to
anything like this extent. Secondly, Kildare's power could not be
destroyed by his removal from the deputyship. Surrey had put
new life into the machinery of the Dublin government and a pro-
English party in the Pale had been encouraged, but everything
was overshadowed by uncertainty about the future; Kildare
might still be restored to power, and while this possibility remained no one was willing to appear too active against him.
Outside the Pale his Irish and Anglo-Irish allies stood firm, and
Surrey had not the resources for an aggressive policy. Of the two
facts thus revealed it was the former which produced the strongest
immediate effect upon Henry, and his unwillingness to spend
money made it impossible for him to take decisive action at this
point. For the next few years he tried to secure his ends more
cheaply by balancing Kildare and his chief Anglo-Irish rival Sir
Piers Butler, earl of Ormonde. It is this which explains the rapid
succession of changes in government. In March 1522, after
Surrey's removal, Ormonde became deputy. In August 1524 he
was suddenly dismissed and Kildare was reappointed. Two
years later both were summoned to England. Kildare was kept
there, under some restraint but not exactly a prisoner, while
retaining the title of deputy; Butler was obliged to give up the

earldom of Ormonde to a rival claimant (Sir Thomas Boleyn) but was compensated with that of Ossory, and was allowed to return to Ireland. In 1528 Kildare, still in England, was dismissed, and Butler became deputy once more, only to be removed again within twelve months.

These rapid changes certainly reduced the influence of the two earls, but they also weakened the government at a time when it was being threatened by a revival of European intrigue in Ireland, a natural result of Henry's aggressive foreign policy. As early as 1523 Desmond had concluded an alliance with the king of France, then at war with England. This had come to nothing; but in 1528 he was negotiating with Henry's new enemy, the Emperor Charles V. It was to meet this danger, not to continue the game of playing off one earl against the other, that Henry dismissed Butler in 1529. In his place Sir William Skeffington, like Poynings a civil servant and an experienced soldier, was sent over with men and money to maintain royal authority. But once again Henry baulked at the expense and as soon as the immediate danger was past Skeffington was recalled and Kildare made deputy once more. There may be some connection between Kildare's reappointment and the fall from power of his old enemy Wolsey; but in the main it was an effort to secure for Ireland a government that would be both reliable and cheap. It was too late for such a policy to succeed. There is no evidence that Kildare was actively disloyal, but he was no longer able to serve the king effectively. His prestige had been irretrievably ruined by the frequent changes of the preceding years. A serious wound which he received in 1532 deprived him of much of his physical and mental vigour. He could no longer control the Irish or even defend Dublin. The one advantage of his rule in Henry's eyes was gone and there was nothing for it but to get rid of him. But the king did not act suddenly, and when Kildare left Ireland in February 1534, in obedience to a royal summons, he was still deputy and was allowed to leave his son Lord Offaly ('Silken Thomas') as lord justice in his place.

The year 1534 is a turning-point in Irish history. We cannot say that Henry now embarked deliberately on a new conquest of Ireland, but in fact, from this time onwards, the English government set itself to extend its authority over the whole country. The process was maintained with varying degrees of intensity and by methods of diplomacy as well as of war, and its primary

purpose was defence rather than aggression; but it led to the
military subjugation of Ireland at the end of Elizabeth's reign.
Probably some such development was inevitable. The Tudor
monarchy could not for ever tolerate the existence of a half-
subdued dependency which, if not controlled by England, might
soon be controlled by England's continental enemies. The
position in 1534 called for action. Kildare could no longer rule
Ireland himself, but unless his power were broken he could make
it impossible for anyone else to do so. It may be that Henry
would, even at this stage, have tried to temporise; but his hand
was forced by the sudden insurrection of Kildare's son, who
burst in upon the council chamber in Dublin, flung down the
sword of office, and disowned his allegiance to the king. Undoubtedly Thomas was moved to this action by the rumours
assiduously spread by the enemies of his family that his father
had been put to death and that he himself would be the next
victim. But affairs had now reached the stage at which the
Geraldines must either defy the royal authority or else submit
to the virtual destruction of their power; considering the character
of Thomas, a proud and fiery young man, and the circumstances
in which he found himself, it was perhaps inevitable that he should
choose the path of violent resistance. The ultimate fate of the
family was not essentially affected by his choice.

The struggle with the Kildare power went on intermittently
for the next six years. Though government forces were small
when the rebellion began, Thomas was in an awkward position.
The citizens of Dublin were hostile, for their interest lay in firm
rule and the maintenance of cross-channel trade, and in face of
their hostility he could not capture the castle. The Butlers were
loyal to the crown and on more than one occasion he was obliged
to divert forces to defend his lands against them. The arrival of
Sir William Skeffington with a strong English force soon deprived
him of effective control over any part of the Pale and compelled
him to rely more than ever on his allies among the native Irish.
The speedy fall of his principal stronghold, Maynooth castle,
before Skeffington's artillery, was a warning that rebels could no
longer rely upon immunity behind their fortifications, and the
execution of most of the garrison showed that the day of easy
pardons had gone. For a time Thomas's allies fell away, and he
himself was captured and sent to England. But after a brief
uneasy peace war broke out again more widely than ever, with

Irish and Anglo-Irish throughout the whole country allied in a
great 'Geraldine league'. This looked an imposing combination,
but there were too many old jealousies and selfish ambitions for
unity to last, and the league soon crumbled under the military
defeats inflicted upon it by Skeffington's successor, Lord Leonard
Grey. By 1540 the struggle was over. Not only was the power of
the Leinster Geraldines broken, but the family was almost
exterminated. The ninth earl had died in prison, 'Silken Thomas'
and five of his uncles had been executed at Tyburn, and the
claimant to the earldom was a twelve-year-old boy in exile in
France.

2. HENRY VIII'S NEW IRISH POLICY

In 1540 Ireland lay open to reconquest. With the disappearance
of the Leinster Geraldines there was, for the time being, no force
capable of resisting the crown. But Henry was not in a position
to use the opportunity. His policy of ecclesiastical nationalism
had raised dangers both at home and abroad and he was unwilling to commit himself too deeply in Ireland. Already the cost
of maintaining government there was considerable. Even at the
end of the reign, when royal authority seemed firmly established
and the country was comparatively peaceful, Ireland was not self-
supporting, but required an annual £5,000 from the English
treasury. There was nothing to spare for large-scale military
undertakings.

Once more, therefore, Henry resolved to get what he could
by diplomatic means, to revert to the 'sober ways, politic drifts
and amiable persuasions' which he had urged Surrey to follow
twenty years earlier. Some beginning had been made already.
In the first interval of the Kildare war a parliament had been
summoned which had obediently enacted for Ireland the most
important of the statutes passed by the 'reformation parliament'
in England. The dissolution of religious houses had also begun
and, as in England, liberal grants of monastic lands helped to
reconcile the magnates (both Anglo-Irish and Irish) to the ecclesiastical changes. It was, perhaps, the ease with which parliament
had been induced to accept Henry's wishes in 1537 that encouraged
him to trust to peaceful methods in exploiting the final victory
over the Leinster Geraldines.

The essence of Henry's policy was that the entire ruling class of

Ireland should be brought into real dependence upon himself. So far as the Anglo-Irish were concerned this meant no more than the application of existing law. But the relationship between the native rulers and the lord of Ireland had always been ill-defined, and some radical change in their position was necessary if they were to form a loyal and active element in the state.

The execution of this policy was entrusted to Sir Anthony St Leger, appointed deputy in 1540 in succession to Lord Leonard Grey. He was well fitted for the task, for he was a soldier, a diplomat and an administrator, and he had already spent several years in Ireland. As a special commissioner from the king he had travelled over much of the country, both inside and outside the Pale, and he had been concerned in the management of parliament.

St Leger set to work by concluding a series of individual agreements with the more important Irish chiefs. Such agreements had long formed part of the regular pattern of Irish politics; but now they were concluded much more widely, and they contained provisions which established a new relationship between the chiefs and the crown. The agreement with Turlough O'Toole in November 1540 was a model for those which followed: he was to surrender his lands to Henry, to receive them back to be held by knight-service, to keep no private forces except with the consent of the deputy, and to use English laws and customs. These conditions formed the essence of the policy of 'surrender and re-grant' which, within the next few years, was applied to almost all Ireland and brought every Irish ruler into formal relationship with the crown. The more powerful of them were given English titles. Conn O'Neill became earl of Tyrone, Murrough O'Brien became earl of Thomond, MacGilpatrick became baron of Upper Ossory, Donough O'Brien became baron of Ibrackin. 'Degenerate English' and rebellious Anglo-Irish returned to their allegiance and received similar treatment. MacWilliam Burke surrendered his lands and received them back with the title of earl of Clanricard; Desmond made public submission to the deputy and received the royal pardon.

The public declaration of the new policy came in June 1541, when a parliament specially summoned for the purpose conferred upon Henry the title 'king of Ireland'. The parliament was unusually well attended, and in addition to the Anglo-Irish ecclesiastics, nobles, gentry and citizens, so many Irish chiefs or their representatives were present that it was thought necessary

to have the bill read over to them in their native language, and
they too expressed their 'liberal consents'. The whole proceeding
was carried through with great enthusiasm, and on the following
Sunday the new title was publicly proclaimed in St Patrick's
cathedral after a solemn mass sung by the archbishop of Dublin.
Thus Henry made it clear that his right to Ireland did not depend
upon papal grant, a ground upon which he could not now logically
stand. The mere change of title meant little. But the dutiful
presence of so many Anglo-Irish nobles and the representatives
of-so many counties, cities and boroughs, outside as well as inside
the Pale, and, above all, the attendance of so many of the native
Irish chiefs, were significant. It seemed as if the conquest was at
last to be completed, not by force but by peaceful agreement.

In this policy Henry showed a more enlightened statesmanship
than many of the Englishmen who have had to govern Ireland.
His main objects were conciliation and fusion: the conciliation
of the great by confirming them in their lands, granting them new
titles and sharing with them the spoil of the religious houses; the
fusion of the colonial and the native populations by a complete
abandonment of the policy of segregation and by the extension
of English law to the whole country. For a time Henry seemed to
have succeeded. There was general submission to his claims.
Anglo-Irish and Irish alike formally recognised him as king of
Ireland and renounced 'the usurped authority of the bishop of
Rome'. Thus the declaration of the kingdom of Ireland and the
royal supremacy over the church were publicly endorsed by the
leaders of the ruling class, native and colonial.

Whatever its merits and however great its temporary success,
this policy failed. The cause is probably to be found, not in any
single factor, but in the cumulative effect of many. The system of
'surrender and re-grant' ignored the Irish law of land tenure, by
which the chief's right in the lands over which he ruled was not
personal and hereditary but official and for life. Conn O'Neill
and other ambitious chiefs were quite ready to accept these royal
grants and to base upon them claims which they pushed to the
utmost, in defiance of Irish law, against their allies and dependants. Thus the rank and file of the Irish gentry found themselves
threatened with deprivation by their own leaders in alliance with
the English king. St Leger had hoped that the new policy, by
establishing the system of primogeniture, would end the chronic
evil of internecine strife, but instead the evil was aggravated.

Within a few years the legal heir to the earldom of Clanricard found himself opposed by a chief elected in the traditional fashion, and a similar dispute in the earldom of Tyrone helped to keep Ulster in a state of civil war for many years.

It is fairly easy to see how this clash of legal systems was likely to affect the success of Henry's policy. There are two other factors whose weight is harder to estimate. The ecclesiastical changes which accompanied the policy have sometimes been regarded as contributory to its failure; but this is only true in so far as these changes prepared the way for the protestantism of Edward VI's reign. The other doubtful factor is the nature of the Irish social system which Henry was trying to recast on peaceful English lines. Irish life was organised for war, not for peace. The Irish chief or Anglo-Irish lord was essentially a war-leader and in every Irish state the most influential class had a vested interest in fighting. In these circumstances it is hard to see how the royal peace could have been permanently imposed on the whole kingdom without a preliminary conquest. This is perhaps the fundamental reason for the failure of Henry's policy. In a sense, it might be regarded as a condemnation of his attempt to proceed by peaceful means; but he can hardly be blamed for not recognising at the time what can be seen clearly only in retrospect.

3. THE REFORMATION

Though Henry VIII's ecclesiastical policy had been accepted in Ireland as readily as in England, the circumstances of the two countries were quite different. The sixteenth-century reformation came to Ireland as an alien movement. There had been little of that intellectual inquiry and criticism which had been growing in other parts of western Christendom; and the Irish church was not strong or rich enough to excite the same degree of jealousy and greed among the secular nobles as was common elsewhere. The weakness and poverty of the church resulted mainly from the discord between English and Irish clergy and from the constant warfare which made the regular collection of ecclesiastical dues almost impossible. In many parts of the country the parish churches and even the cathedrals were in ruins, and benefices were often vacant or held by absentees, so that the people had to depend for spiritual ministrations upon 'the poor friars beggars', and the popular influence which the friars thus acquired was later of great importance. Nowhere was there any general interest in those questions of faith and order which dominated theological thought in Germany, France and Britain.

Though Ireland was thus unprepared for the protestant reformation, it was not likely to offer serious resistance to Henry's policy of 'catholicism without the pope'. The native Irish rulers had no reason for supporting papal authority, which had generally been exerted on the side of the English; the Anglo-Irish might naturally be expected to fall in line with a policy which had already been accepted in England. And this is in fact what happened. There was, to begin with, some opposition among the Anglo-Irish clergy, led by Archbishop Cromer of Armagh, and in the parliament of 1536–7 the clerical proctors raised some objections, which led to the final exclusion of the lower clergy from the Irish parliament. But when once the act of supremacy had been passed, the majority of the bishops seem to have conformed and the secular magnates made no bones about renouncing papal authority. It is true that the Geraldine party, both before and after the passing of the act of supremacy, used religion as a rallying cry. But this was due to the hope of securing foreign help at least as much as to conviction, and in the end none of the rebels hesitated to accept the royal supremacy as a condition of pardon. The apathy of the native Irish in the whole question shows very clearly in the failure of the Jesuit missionaries who arrived in Ulster in 1542 with letters from the pope and from Ignatius Loyola. The northern chiefs gave them such a scant welcome that they were soon glad to make their escape to Scotland. The attitude of bishops and secular magnates had little effect upon the opinion of the common people, who were strongly influenced against the royal supremacy by the preaching of the friars; but for the time being Henry seemed to have succeeded and the danger of a popular opposition had not yet appeared.

So far, the course of the ecclesiastical revolution in Ireland had been almost exactly parallel with that in England. But with the attempt to use the royal supremacy to bring about changes in doctrine and liturgy the difference between the two countries at once appeared. Not only was there no strong reform party in Ireland to counter the inevitable opposition, but the changes came at a time when the country was entering upon a new period of political unrest. The weaknesses in Henry VIII's system of

government have already been pointed out, and in the decade
following his death these were aggravated by frequent changes in
English policy and by the outbreak of war with France and the
consequent activity of French envoys in Ireland. The superficial
peace established by the policy of 'surrender and re-grant' disappeared in a series of Irish insurrections and the defence of the
Pale again became one of the deputy's main preoccupations.

It was in these most unfavourable circumstances that the
government of Edward VI set about extending to Ireland the
ecclesiastical changes that had already taken place in England.
No Irish parliament was summoned and there was no formal
synod or convocation of the clergy; but an edition of the English
Book of Common Prayer of 1549 was printed in Dublin (the
first book to be printed in Ireland) and its use enjoined by virtue
of the royal prerogative. Except in the Pale and in a few cities and
towns beyond it the government's policy had little effect. Over the
greater part of the country church services went on as before.
Even within the Pale the change was by no means universally
acquiesced in; everywhere, among both Irish and Anglo-Irish,
there was a strong spirit of opposition, and the few enthusiastic
reformers among the bishops found little support. Many of the
bishops and temporal rulers who had accepted the royal supremacy
under Henry VIII were now ready, as in England, to return to
papal authority as a necessary defence against doctrinal inno-
vation. Such was George Dowdall, Henry's archbishop of
Armagh and a strong supporter of royal supremacy in the
church. He went into exile rather than accept the Book of Common Prayer, for 'he would never be a bishop where the holy mass
was abolished'. Within a short time he had been reconciled with
the papacy and was reappointed to his see by papal provision.

The reversal of policy which followed hard upon the death of
Edward VI was almost universally welcomed in Ireland. As in
England, the reforming bishops were deprived. But no pro-
ceedings were taken against them for heresy, and the fires of
Smithfield and Oxford, which lit the way for a protestant settlement in England, had no counterpart in Ireland. No doubt this
arose mainly from the fact that there were so few protestants
that there was no need to burn them; but it reflects also the
difficulties of a government which had other and more urgent
problems to attend to. Neither the attempted introduction of
protestantism nor its abandonment had produced any funda-

mental change in the political situation, and in civil affairs Mary
simply continued the policy of Edward VI. The formal restoration of papal authority did nothing to reconcile the native Irish
to English rule and her reign was almost wholly occupied in
military operations against them.

When Elizabeth succeeded to the throne it was inevitable that
she should extend to Ireland the protestant policy which circumstances had compelled her to adopt in England. But she was
anxious that the continuity of government should be maintained
and it was Mary's deputy, Lord Fitzwalter, whom she reappointed,
with the title of earl of Sussex, to carry out the task. As in England,
the church settlement was a parliamentary one, and it was based
mainly upon acts of supremacy and uniformity almost identical
with those passed in England. The parliament which passed them
met in Dublin in January 1560 and was dissolved barely three
weeks later. The speed with which such controversial measures
were got through, in spite of very strong opposition, has been
used as an argument in favour of the theory that they were either
passed by a trick or not passed at all but simply added to the
statute book. The truth probably is that the members, elected
under government supervision, carried out, however reluctantly,
government policy. The number of bishops present at the parliament is uncertain; but the bishops in general made no public
opposition to the acts and only two of them openly refused to take
the oath of supremacy. Nevertheless, the act of uniformity was
not—indeed could not be—generally enforced, and acceptance
of the royal supremacy did not necessarily mean acceptance of
the Book of Common Prayer.

The legislation of 1560 marks the formal close of the Irish
reformation. But in another sense it is only a beginning, for the
reformed church had as yet few adherents in any part of the
country. Even in the Pale Elizabeth dared not risk alienating the
loyal Anglo-Irish by a rigid enforcement of the act of uniformity,
and throughout a great part of the country the government had
not the means of doing so even if it had desired. If little could be
done by force not much was accomplished by persuasion. The
bishops and clergy in general showed no missionary zeal, and
various projects for publishing the Bible and prayer book in
Irish were postponed until it was too late. For the field of enterprise thus neglected by the reformed clergy was soon seized upon

by the Jesuits and missionary priests from the continent whose labours, supplementing those of the friars, laid the foundation of that devotion to the Roman catholic faith which has long been characteristic of the bulk of the population of Ireland.

In Elizabeth's reign, also, the political consequences of the reformation began to appear. The papacy, for so long the ally of English power in Ireland, now became its enemy, and a religious bitterness was added to the old struggle. This change complicated the position of the Anglo-Irish—the 'Old English' as they came to be called to distinguish them from the new colonists of the Tudor period. The bulk of them refused to accept the reformation and so far they had a common ground with the vast majority of the native Irish. In Munster and Connaught this went a long way towards completing the fusion of the two races; but the Old English of the Pale were traditionally loyal to the English connection and to them the natives had always been the enemy. This loyalty survived almost unimpaired through the reign of Elizabeth. But outside the Pale a slowly growing national senti- ment came to be identified with the cause of the papacy; and when the material interests as well as the religious freedom of the Old English were threatened under the first two Stuarts even those of the Pale threw in their lot with the majority.

4. ELIZABETH AND IRELAND

Religious differences have played such an influential part in Irish politics during the last three and a half centuries that there has been a natural tendency to exaggerate the immediate political results of the reformation. The truth is that the basic continuity of Tudor policy was not affected by the change. Its great object, surviving all ecclesiastical fluctuations, was to make sure that Ireland should not become a centre of intrigue for English rebels or continental enemies. Despite the fact that it issued in military conquest Tudor policy in Ireland was essentially defensive.

Elizabeth succeeded to the throne at a moment when the danger from Ireland seemed particularly acute. Sussex warned her how easy it would be for a foreign power 'aided by civil faction' to get a footing in the country, and prophesied that the result would be 'such a ruin to England as I am afeard to think on'. But shortage of money and the precariousness of her position at home compelled Elizabeth to act cautiously. Fortunately for her, France was too deeply concerned in Scottish affairs to pay much attention to Ireland, and Philip of Spain was still disposed to be conciliatory. This easing of the tension enabled Elizabeth to play a waiting game. The chief source of unrest was in Ulster, where the settlement made by Henry VIII had completely broken down. Conn O'Neill, earl of Tyrone, died in 1559 and the Irish, ignoring the English title and English law of succession, elected his younger son, Shane, as 'The O'Neill'. This was a plain defiance of royal authority, but the government had not the resources necessary for direct military action. Negotiations with Shane went on for years. But though he paid a visit to England and made public submission to the queen, he returned to Ireland as free as he left it and continued to rule in virtual independence. For the time being, the government allowed the Tyrone earldom to lapse.

Shane O'Neill was one of the last of the great Gaelic chieftains. He was a courageous soldier but not a great commander, a clever negotiator, but a short-sighted diplomat; his conception of government was purely personal and his ambition was limited to the establishment of the military supremacy of the O'Neills in Ulster. It was the reckless pursuit of this ambition which led to his downfall. His two main rivals were the O'Donnells of Tyrconnell and the Scottish settlers, MacDonnells from the western isles, who had been for some time establishing themselves in north-east Ulster. The government took advantage of this rivalry to turn O'Neill against the Scots and O'Donnell against O'Neill. For some years Shane was unexpectedly victorious, but in 1567 he was completely overthrown by the O'Donnells. The Scots, to whom he fled for refuge, killed him and sent his head to the deputy. This sudden reversal presented an opportunity which Elizabeth refused to take; once the immediate danger from Ulster was gone she fell back on a policy of defence. Shane's cousin and tanist, Turlough, was allowed to succeed him in peace, with formal recognition as 'chief of his name and nation'. He was an unadventurous ruler, satisfied to hold on quietly to what he had, and though a couple of years later the Irish parliament passed an act of attainder against Shane and confiscated his lands, Turlough was, in fact, left alone. The only important step which the government took was the establishment of Hugh O'Neill, Conn's grandson and the claimant to the earldom of Tyrone, in part of the

O'Neill lands, with his father's title of baron of Dungannon.[1] Hugh's ambition went far beyond this but adversity had taught him caution and infinite patience; for more than twenty years he watched and waited, and when, at last, he threw all on the fortunes of war it was rather to defend what he held than in the hope of making any fresh conquest.

Ulster was cut off from the rest of the country by a natural barrier of mountain and lake and its remoteness discouraged European intervention. So long as the northern chiefs were quiescent it was safe enough to leave them alone. But Munster presented a different sort of problem. Contacts with the Pale were much closer, and the great Anglo-Irish lords who dominated much of the province were uneasy at the government's ecclesiastical policy, cautiously carried out though it was. Above all, the southern ports were in regular communication with Europe and offered easy entry to England's continental enemies. In these circumstances it was a matter of mere necessity to establish effective control over Munster. This might have been accomplished with no more than sporadic resistance had it not been for the determined character of one man, James FitzMaurice Fitz-Gerald,[2] cousin of the earl of Desmond and the most able representative of the Munster Geraldines. The relative importance of the family had been increased by the overthrow of the Kildare branch, but the nominal head of it at this time, Gerald, the fifteenth earl, was a man of weak character, untrustworthy, oppressive and selfishly ambitious, without the strength of will to pursue any consistent policy. In 1567 he was arrested and sent over to England, and James FitzMaurice was left to look after his interests. FitzMaurice was a fanatical opponent of protestantism and of the English government, and it was his aim to build up a Roman catholic alliance among the Irish and Anglo-Irish of Munster.

Religious motives alone would hardly have produced a rebellion; but every land-holder in Munster was alarmed, at this time, for the security of his title, despite the settlement made by Henry VIII. FitzMaurice played upon these fears, and the detention of Desmond in England seemed to justify suspicion of the government's honesty. In these circumstances he gained

1. Hugh's father, Matthew, though illegitimate, had been recognised by Henry VIII as Conn's heir, and had been created baron of Dungannon.
2. Usually referred to as James FitzMaurice.

many supporters and began his revolt in the summer of 1569. His own enthusiasm gave it something of the character of a crusade, an aspect which he naturally stressed in his appeals to the pope and to the king of Spain. The publication, early in 1570, of the papal bull *Regnans in excelsis*[1] may have increased the religious zeal of the rebels, but it brought them no practical aid and it complicated their political position. The king of Spain sent a small supply of arms, but no men and little money. Within a short time the military successes of the English enabled them to take effective measures for the restoration of order. The most important step in this direction was the establishment of a new system of government for Munster. A president was appointed with extensive authority over the province and with a council and court of his own. The first president, Sir John Perrot, fought and governed vigorously. He soon deprived FitzMaurice of effective control over any extensive territory and in January 1572 compelled him to submit.

As in Ulster, once the immediate threat had been averted the government relaxed its efforts. Desmond was allowed to retain his earldom and to return to Ireland, and FitzMaurice was set at liberty. But the relaxation was more apparent than real, for Perrot continued to work effectively for the establishment of English law and it was clear that the old semi-independence of the Munster lords was drawing to an end. FitzMaurice did not abandon his intrigues, but soon realised that nothing could be accomplished without foreign aid. In 1575 he escaped to the continent where he spent his time 'running from one papist prince to another with the pope's commendations' and trying to gather an army for the invasion of Ireland. At length, in 1579, he landed at Dingle with a mixed force of some 300 Italians and Spaniards financed by the pope and the king of Spain. With him came Nicholas Sanders, an Englishman, as papal nuncio, whose presence emphasised still further the religious aspect of the undertaking, upon which FitzMaurice had from the start laid so much stress.

The war that followed was not one of battles but of skirmishes, ambushes and sieges. Elizabeth would not afford either men or money to make a speedy end, nor did the nature of the country make such a policy easy. The rebels were constantly sustained,

1. This was the bull in which Pope Pius V declared Elizabeth excommunicate and her subjects released from their obedience.

despite reverses, by the hope of Spanish help. But when help did
come, in November 1580, it proved of little use. A force of 600
Spaniards landed at Smerwick, fortified the town and waited to
see what would happen. The rebels were just as dilatory; but the
deputy, Lord Grey de Wilton, acted at once. He assembled every
man he could spare, marched against Smerwick, compelled the
Spaniards to surrender at discretion and put them all to the
sword. But this very success helped to prolong the war; for
Elizabeth, convinced that no more Spanish troops would be
sent, cut down supplies and left the deputy to bring the war to a
lingering end with reduced forces. The fighting dragged on for
another three years and almost all Munster was laid waste. The
cruelties committed by both sides were such as naturally occur in a
struggle between an organised army and elusive guerilla forces
which have the sympathy of the countryside and which cannot
or will not fight pitched battles. Both sides suffered from shortage
of supplies, but the rebels also lacked effective leadership. Fitz-
Maurice was killed in a skirmish with the Burkes a month after
his landing; he was succeeded by Sir John of Desmond, the
earl's brother, who was killed in 1581, and in the same year
Sanders died of hunger and dysentery. The earl of Desmond
himself, without plan or principle, could do little to hold his
supporters together; but the prestige of his position counted for
something, and his death in November 1583 was the signal for
general submission. The Munster rebellion was over.

The religious aspect of the rebellion was significant, for it
marked a step towards the union of native Irish and Old English
against the government on the basis of their common faith. Such
a union was never completely accomplished, and at this stage
long-standing racial and family rivalries often counted for more
than religious affinities. In Munster not only the Butlers and their
allies but many of the native Irish remained loyal to the queen.
In the Pale, and in the Anglo-Irish towns throughout the country,
though there was some sympathy with the rebels, loyalty was the
rule. But the general effect of the war was to sharpen the political
barrier between protestantism and Roman catholicism, to
strengthen the government's conviction that the latter was
synonymous with treason, and so to prepare the way for a systematic politico-religious persecution.

Though Elizabeth had been forced into the Munster war by the
need for guarding Ireland against invasion, her own policy had

already made an armed clash with the old order almost inevitable.
Henry VIII, faced with hostility both at home and abroad, had embarked on a policy of anglicisation, and his successors had little
choice but to follow his example. But every strengthening of royal
authority, every extension of English law, however necessary to
the security of the kingdom, was a threat to their independence
which the Irish and Anglo-Irish magnates were almost bound to
resist. In these circumstances Henry's system of 'surrender and
re-grant' broke down, and in Mary's reign the first experiment
was made in establishing 'plantations'. Mary's plantations were
in Leix and Offaly, renamed Queen's County and King's County,
and though they failed the idea was not abandoned. A new
attempt in Ulster, after the formal confiscation of Shane
O'Neill's lands, was costly, but no more successful. In spite of
this, the government decided to take the opportunity presented
by the end of the Munster rebellion to embark on an even more
elaborate scheme. England was beginning to feel the need of an
outlet for her population, and the idea of such organised plantations, combining state direction with private enterprise, seems to
have appealed to the Tudor mind. The various Irish projects of
this and the succeeding century are linked with the general
movement towards overseas expansion; that which Burghley and
Walsingham drew up for Munster was based in part upon
Raleigh's proposals for Virginia, and Raleigh himself, his half-
brother Sir Humphrey Gilbert, with others of less note, were
engaged in plantation enterprises both in Ireland and America.

In Ireland the main object of the plantation policy was to
substitute loyal English settlers for disloyal Irish or Anglo-Irish.
About 400,000 acres of land confiscated after the Munster
rebellion was to be divided into 'seignories', varying in size from
4,000 to 12,000 acres. These were to be granted to English 'undertakers' who were to plant them with English-born families. The
management of the whole affair was incompetent and slow, the
necessary surveying was inaccurately done and years passed
between the making of grants and the actual establishment of
the grantees in possession. A commission of inquiry in 1592
found that of fifty-eight undertakers only thirteen were resident
and that there were only 245 English families on the planted
lands. This comparative failure was due partly to incompetence,
partly to the readiness with which undertakers, anxious for quick
returns, accepted Irish tenants at high rents, in spite of their

agreement to bring in English. But an even more important
reason was the havoc which three or four years of bitter fighting
had produced in Munster. Famine and disease, as well as war,
had depopulated the country, and the new settlement was
scarcely beginning to be profitable when it was practically swept
away in the great insurrection of 1598. Four years later, when
Raleigh sold his Munster estate of 42,000 acres it was said to be
costing him £200 a year in upkeep.

Though Elizabeth was ready, when occasion offered, to follow
Mary's policy of military conquest secured by plantation, she was
also ready to continue and adapt her father's more peaceful methods.
It was in this way that she set about extending effective royal
authority over Connaught. In 1585 a commission was appointed
to report on the rights and holdings of all the Anglo-Irish and
Irish lords and chiefs of the province, and on the basis of this
report a settlement was made. Each landholder was confirmed
in his estate, with a new title good in English law, and in return
was to pay a quit-rent to the crown. Existing feudal and Irish
services due from tenant to lord were abolished and money rents
substituted. Old Irish family titles, such as 'O'Connor Don' and
'O'Connor Sligo', were prohibited. Succession by primogeniture
was established. Connaught thus escaped the plantation policy
which affected so much of the rest of Ireland; but though the
people remained undisturbed, the Gaelic way of life, so closely
bound up with personal services and with family rather than
territorial titles, was seriously undermined. This 'composition of
Connaught' was to have been confirmed in parliament, but this
was not done, and in the reign of Charles I Wentworth was able
to call the whole settlement in question.

Thus, by a combination of force and diplomacy, and urged on
by fear rather than ambition, Elizabeth extended her authority
over a wider area of Ireland than had been effectively controlled
by any previous English sovereign. The medieval administrative
system was expanded and modified to meet the new situation.
Old counties were revived and new ones established. By 1585
almost all Ireland outside Ulster had been reduced to shire
ground, and even Ulster had been shired on paper. The presidency
system in Munster and Connaught performed much the same
function as the English Council of the North and Council of
Wales. The court of Castle Chamber in Dublin dealt with the
same sort of cases as the court of Star Chamber in England. But

the similarity between the English and Irish governmental systems was not so close as this comparison might suggest. The English government was of natural growth and rested upon the implicit consent of the people; in Ireland the very notion of effective central authority had been imposed from outside, the independence of local magnates had still be to reckoned with, and government relied directly upon military force.

The difference in spirit between the two systems becomes clear when we consider the part played by the Irish parliament. Throughout Elizabeth's reign it met only three times in all. The first of these meetings, in 1560, was concerned almost exclusively with the ecclesiastical settlement and lasted for less than four weeks. The second parliament, in 1569, was that which attainted Shane O'Neill. Here, for the first time, two parties emerge fairly clearly: the government or 'court' party, consisting mainly of officials and of nominees of the deputy, returned by counties, cities and boroughs under royal control, and an opposition party made up of Anglo-Irish gentry. The life of this parliament was brief and the struggle between the parties did not come to a head over any major issue; but the government was uneasy at the strength of the opposition and did not call parliament again until 1585, when it was felt desirable to have acts of attainder passed against the leaders of the Munster rebellion. The membership of the lower house in this parliament reflected the expansion of royal power: there were members from twenty-seven counties and thirty-six cities and boroughs, so that, territorially at least, almost the whole kingdom was represented; but a racial exclusiveness remained, for the members were almost without exception English by birth or descent, either new settlers or old colonists. Once again, two parties emerged and the line of division was now clearly religious. The opposition was made up of 'recusants' (i.e. those who refused to take the oath of supremacy) and was strong enough to defeat proposed government legislation against the Jesuits. But most of the other measures put forward by the government, including the acts of attainder, got through. Despite this degree of success Elizabeth did not summon the Irish parliament again.

From this brief account of the Irish parliament under Elizabeth three points emerge. First, it was called only to deal with special topics and formed no regular part of the governmental system. Secondly, it was essentially a 'loyal' body: the opposition attacked

certain aspects of government policy, but they stood fast by the
authority of the English crown and were quite ready to attaint
rebels. Thirdly, the existence of a constitutional opposition,
though it was a check on the government, was a step towards
establishing general peace. If all the opposition elements in the
country could be drawn within the parliamentary system they
would no longer be a threat to peace and security. But events
showed that this could not be brought about save by an extension
of military conquest.

5. HUGH O'NEILL AND THE END OF GAELIC RESISTANCE

During the ten years which followed the end of the Munster
war Ireland enjoyed an unwonted peace. The power and prestige
of the government expanded. The danger of Spanish intervention
was at least checked by the overthrow of the armada in 1588.
The established church showed signs of more vigorous life, and
the setting up of a university in Dublin (Trinity College) in 1591
promised a more plentiful supply of well-trained and zealous
clergy. At no previous point had the progressive anglicisation of
the whole country seemed so likely. In retrospect, one can see
that the very prospect of such a development might well bring
on a struggle with Ulster, the last great stronghold of Gaelic
tradition; but, at the time, the position in Ulster seemed safe
enough. The government's protégé, Hugh O'Neill, who was
steadily building up his influence, maintained at least a formal
loyalty. He had served in person against the Munster rebels and
he had attended the parliament of 1585, in which his claim to the
earldom of Tyrone had been recognised. A couple of years later
he had received further grants of land from the queen. Yet it was
round Hugh O'Neill that the opposition of Ulster, and most of
Ireland, was to gather.

Hugh was more subtle and more far-sighted than his uncle
Shane, but his outlook was not essentially different. He was an
O'Neill: his first ambition was to secure recognition as 'chief of
his name and nation' and thereafter to establish O'Neill supremacy
in Ulster. But he realised, as Shane had never done, the need for
caution. Instead of defying his cousin Turlough, Shane's successor, he persuaded him to give up his position peaceably, and
in 1593 Hugh himself took the title of 'The O'Neill'. Instead of
trying to crush all rival powers in the north he made a firm

alliance with the chief of the O'Donnells, Hugh Roe. Both actions
were alarming to the government, for the native title was, strictly
speaking, illegal, and Hugh Roe O'Donnell was bitterly anti-
English. It need not be supposed, however, that O'Neill's previous
professions of loyalty were entirely insincere. He was quite
prepared to be loyal so long as his loyalty did not clash with his
personal ambition. But if he was to be recognised by his countrymen as chief of his name he must take the traditional title. To
be 'earl of Tyrone' meant very little in Ulster; to be 'The O'Neill'
meant almost everything. Again, he must either fight Hugh Roe
or make friends with him, and there can be no doubt about the
wisdom of his choice. He was not preparing for aggression, but
merely for the defence of what he considered his rights. And the
need for such defence seemed to be increasing. Although the
government had not deliberately embarked on a complete conquest it was becoming clear that anglicisation could not stop short
at the borders of Ulster. Already in 1591 a land settlement in
Monaghan, similar to that in Connaught, had undermined the
traditional way of life there. The establishment of military
garrisons at various strategic points suggested that the ground
was being prepared for a general assault upon the north.

The truth is that both sides acted out of fear. The government
was alarmed at the growing power and independence of O'Neill
and could not ignore the possibility of a new Spanish attack,
with Ulster instead of Munster as its first object. O'Neill and
O'Donnell saw the Gaelic tradition being gradually eaten away
in the rest of Ireland and they looked forward with dismay to the
prospect of English law and the reformed church being imposed
upon Ulster also. The lament of a southern bard over the fallen
state of the O'Byrnes reflects the natural horror of an aristocratic
society at the levelling tendency of the English legal system:

Torment it is to me that in the very tribal gatherings foreigners
proscribe them that are Ireland's royal chiefs, in whose own ancestral
territory is vouchsafed them now no designation other than the lowly
wood-kerne's name.[1]

In this uneasy position casual armed clashes led naturally to a
general struggle. There was some desultory fighting in 1594, in
which O'Donnell and some of the lesser chiefs were involved.

1. S. H. O Grady, *Catalogue of Irish MSS. in the British Museum*, i. 505.

In the following spring Hugh O'Neill himself took the field. The war which followed soon acquired something of a national character, but it began because Hugh O'Neill felt that his position in Ulster was threatened.

The government made the initial mistake of supposing that Hugh could be dealt with as easily as Shane had been, and that the alliance of the northern chiefs would soon break up. They were therefore ready to make terms and to follow delaying tactics, believing that time was in their favour. But Hugh's position became stronger instead of weaker, and in August 1598 the whole situation was changed by his crushing defeat of the English commander, Sir Henry Bagenal, at the battle of the Yellow Ford. The effects of the battle were felt throughout Ireland. In Connaught, the Burkes now joined the rebels; in Munster, a general insurrection swept away almost every trace of the recent plantation; throughout Leinster, even on the borders of the Pale, the native Irish—the O'Connors, the O'Mores, the O'Byrnes, and the rest—rose in revolt. The battle of the Yellow Ford threatened to turn an Ulster insurrection into a national war in which the bond of a common religion would link Irish and Anglo-Irish under the elected leader of the most illustrious of the ancient royal houses of Ireland.

But the position was neither so simple nor so favourable for O'Neill as might at first appear. Some of the native Irish rulers still held to the crown. In Munster, though an earl of Desmond was found to revive the claims and alliances of his family, Ormonde stood fast, a centre of loyal resistance. The towns, both in the Pale and throughout the south and west, remained in the hands of the government. Once O'Neill ventured out of Ulster they were a constant menace to his communications and they made it impossible for him or his allies to establish a firm grip on the country. Above all, the lords and gentry of the Pale, though recusants for the most part, continued to support the crown. But the weaknesses in O'Neill's position were not immediately obvious and the government was shaken out of its usual complacency by the magnitude of the danger. An independent Ireland in alliance with Spain would threaten the whole structure of English power, based as it was upon command of the sea. From this time onwards men and money were poured into Ireland on an unprecedented scale and the policy of petty economies and makeshift expedients was abandoned.

Almost as soon as the news of O'Neill's victory and its results
reached England the government there set to work to prepare a
new army. The command was entrusted to the earl of Essex and
in April 1599 he arrived in Ireland with almost 20,000 men. But
though Essex was a good soldier he had not the qualities necessary
for Irish warfare. He frittered away his resources and instead of
attacking O'Neill at once allowed him to negotiate. Essex's
failure led directly to his own downfall and he was replaced by a
commander of a different stamp—Charles Blount, Lord Mountjoy. Mountjoy arrived in Ireland with a carefully-worked-out
plan of campaign which was eventually to bring O'Neill to
destruction. He resolved to avoid pitched battles, to strengthen
existing garrisons and establish new ones, to destroy crops and
cattle, to cut off O'Neill's sources of supply, and so to wear him
out. It is a method by which well-equipped and well-supplied
forces have rarely failed to defeat an irregular enemy, however
courageous, and on this occasion, though success came slowly, it
came surely. The first great blow to O'Neill was the establishment
of a fort at Derry. This could be maintained by sea and it was a
constant threat to his rear; from Derry, also, other garrisons
were planted throughout the north and thus his communications,
even within his own country, were endangered.

O'Neill's position was now a precarious one. He had gained no
permanent advantage from his great victory of 1598, for the
insurrections in Munster and Connaught had flickered out. He
could not maintain himself indefinitely in Ulster, the time for
negotiation had passed, and his one chance lay in the arrival of
substantial foreign help. But when help did come it proved useless.
In September 1601 a Spanish fleet, with 4,000 troops on board,
reached Kinsale. They received little reinforcement from the
neighbouring population, they made no attempt to advance
inland, and were soon closely besieged by an English army.
Three years earlier, in the first flush of the victory of the Yellow
Ford, the arrival of such a force might have turned the scale;
now, it offered no more than a last desperate hope. O'Neill and
O'Donnell marched south with all the troops they could raise.
They encamped near Kinsale and established communications
with the Spaniards; but an attempt at combined action, which was
meant to take the English by surprise, failed completely and the
Irish were heavily defeated. O'Neill retreated to the north,
O'Donnell took ship for Spain, and the Spaniards surrendered

Kinsale on terms which left them free to return home. The war
dragged on for more than a year longer; but O'Neill, forced back
finally on Ulster and deprived of his allies, was fighting now for
terms, not for victory.

Elizabeth did not live to see the end. O'Neill's final submission, in March 1603, took place six days after her death, and
it was James I who settled the conditions upon which the defeated
chiefs were to live. In appearance, these were generous enough.
At the time of his submission O'Neill had given up his native
title and abjured foreign alliances; James allowed him to retain
the earldom of Tyrone and confirmed him in most of the lands
granted to his grandfather Conn in 1542. Rory, younger brother
of Hugh O'Donnell, was made earl of Tyrconnell. Other chiefs
who had been in rebellion were given similar terms according to
their rank. There were no stipulations about religion. In form,
the settlement differed little from others made or proposed at
various stages during the long struggle between Tudor England
and the Irish kings, and many of those who had suffered in the
cause of government complained that O'Neill had got more by
rebellion than they by loyalty. But in fact O'Neill was beaten.
Generous terms were possible because he was no longer dangerous
and his inactivity during the next few years shows that he knew
it. What he still held he held by grace of the king and not in his
own strength.

With the surrender of Hugh O'Neill the Tudor conquest was
complete. The social and political system of Gaelic Ireland was
gone; the traditional authority of the chief and the rights assured
under the brehon law were replaced by the authority of the
Dublin government and the common law of England. Gaelic
society was aristocratic: it was the chiefs and their privileged
dependants who suffered most from the change and whose
downfall fills the laments of the professional bards. For the
labouring population the new order may well have been in some
respects beneficial; but there was little likelihood that they would
become reconciled to it. The Gaelic language long survived the
destruction of the Gaelic social system, keeping alive the traditions of the past, and setting a barrier between the mass of the
population and their new rulers. It was even more important
that the religious distinction had by this time become stable;
and though Mountjoy's victories enabled the reformed church

to expand its authority in the north there was little or no change
in the ecclesiastical allegiance of the people. Despite its military
completeness, the Tudor conquest left a foundation for continuing
resistance to English power.

During the long-drawn-out wars of conquest the country had
been systematically wasted by both sides, and contemporary
accounts give a very gloomy picture of Ireland at the end of
Elizabeth's reign. But Irish rural economy, perhaps because it
was simple, had the power of rapid recovery, and wealth increased
during the peaceful period which followed the accession of James
I. But the political changes brought about by conquest had a
permanent effect on the economic life of the country. Up to the
middle of the sixteenth century a great part of Ireland's commercial wealth was concentrated in the ports of the south and
west, which traded with the continent, and especially with
Spain. Some of them, Galway above all, maintained a virtual
independence of the crown, though their populations were
largely English, or Anglo-Norman, in blood and tradition. Now,
with royal authority extending over the whole kingdom, their
former freedom was gone, and though their overseas trade did
not disappear, the tightening of the English connection naturally
increased the relative importance of Dublin and Drogheda and
the other ports on the east coast, well placed as they were for
commerce with England. This increasing Anglo-Irish trade
formed one of the main supports of the new 'English interest'
which was establishing itself in Ireland and which was to complicate so bitterly the civil strife of the mid-seventeenth century.

3

IRELAND IN THE SEVENTEENTH CENTURY

I. THE EARLY STUARTS

With the accession of James I Irish history entered upon a new phase. The last centre of Gaelic particularism had been destroyed and the whole country lay open for the firm establishment of royal authority—the 'kingdom of Ireland' had at last become a reality. Various factors seemed to promise peace and well-being. The union of England, Scotland and Ireland under one crown secured a greater degree of stability in the politics of the British Isles. James showed that he did not mean to press the English victory beyond the point of necessary security: not only were O'Neill and O'Donnell confirmed in their estates but an act of oblivion removed the fear that prosecutions against former rebels might be renewed. The conclusion of peace with Spain in 1604 helped the development of overseas trade, while the increasingly effective enforcement of internal order provided one of the necessary conditions of prosperity at home. The outlook for English power in Ireland and for the general economic improvement of the country seemed brighter in 1603 than for centuries before. But a generation later these pleasing prospects were destroyed in the insurrection of 1641.

The failure of the early Stuart monarchy in Ireland has sometimes been attributed to the tyranny or mismanagement of Wentworth, and sometimes to the internal complications of English politics. But its roots ran far into the past, and the final breach between Charles I and the English parliament was the result and not the cause of insurrection in Ireland. The truth is that the completion of the conquest had simply transferred from the military to the political sphere the great problems of Irish government and of Anglo-Irish relations; but since in the circumstances of the early seventeenth century a political solution of these problems was almost unattainable the renewal of war could hardly be avoided. The difficulties with which Charles I had to contend in Great Britain and the nature of Wentworth's government in Ireland undoubtedly affected the course of events, but could not alter the general pattern. That pattern was mainly determined by the internal conflict of interests which the previous history of Ireland had produced, complicated by those problems of religion and land which in one form or another were to vex Irish political life for centuries to come.

At the beginning of the seventeenth century native Irish chiefs, though deprived of political independence, still held a considerable proportion of the country as landlords by English law. The Old English had a dominant position among the nobles and gentry of Leinster and Munster, and in most of the cities and boroughs. These two groups were mainly Roman catholic, and together they formed the bulk of the landowning and trading classes. But there was also an English population of more recent settlement, made up largely of government officials and their dependants, who had already acquired a good deal of landed property and were constantly on the alert for more. They were mainly if not exclusively protestant and formed the backbone of the established church. The government naturally desired to enlarge this element in the population and for this purpose revived and extended the sixteenth-century policy of plantation.

The most extensive and by far the most successful effort in this direction was the plantation in Ulster. The opportunity was provided by the event always known in Irish history as 'the flight of the earls'. The 'earls' were Tyrone and Tyrconnell, who had never become reconciled to the position in which the war against Elizabeth had left them. Though established in vast estates they could not but feel that their real power was gone with their Irish titles and their political independence. They suspected, with some justice, that many influential government officials were hostile to them and jealous of the liberal treatment they had received. But whether they feared the effect of this hostility on their position in Ireland or hoped to gain foreign help for a renewal of the struggle does not appear. All that is certain is

C

that they secretly obtained a ship and left Ireland in September 1607 with a considerable body of their allies and dependants. They received scant welcome and no help on the continent, until they came to Rome, and they made no effort at any military adventure. But their going left the greater part of Ulster open to confiscation, and the government resolved to seize the opportunity. The secret departure of the earls was regarded as evidence of treason, and the whole area over which they had exercised or claimed lordship was declared forfeit to the crown. This area consisted of the six counties of Armagh, Cavan, Coleraine (now Londonderry), Donegal, Fermanagh, Tyrone. Most, but not all, of the native landlords who had held under Tyrone or Tyrconnell were deprived of their estates. Great areas were handed over to English and Scots 'undertakers' on condition that they planted their estates with British settlers. Other areas went to 'servitors', men who had served the crown in Ireland, who were allowed to take Irish instead of British tenants. There was thus a general change in the ownership of land; but, contrary to the government's intention, there was no large-scale removal of the native population. In each of the planted counties there were certain areas from which, according to the plantation scheme, the natives were to be removed completely, but in fact this was never done. The difficulty of bringing in English and Scots made the new owners quite ready to ignore the conditions imposed by the government and accept the existing occupants, some of whom, of course, were the former landlords, as their tenants. A great share in the settlement was taken by the corporation of London, after which the county and city of Londonderry are named; and the direct interest in Irish affairs which London thus acquired helped to complicate relations with the crown in the reign of Charles I. The progress of the plantation was slow, but the foundations were more firmly laid than in the Munster plantation of Elizabeth's reign, and the steady infiltration of colonists, and especially of lowland Scots, gradually built up a British and protestant population in the north. By 1628, however, there were only about 2,000 British families in the six planted counties.

The two counties of Antrim and Down were not included in the general confiscation, but considerable parts of them had been taken into the king's hands on other grounds and granted to various English and Scottish settlers, even before the main plantation had been begun. In this way the families of Hill,

Montgomery and Hamilton, with many others of less note, established themselves in north-east Ulster, and laid the foundations of the strong Anglo-Scottish protestantism which is still characteristic of the area. The older Scottish settlers, the Mac-Donnells, were confirmed in their lands in north Antrim; but their traditions were Roman catholic and Gaelic, and they did not mingle readily with their new neighbours.

These plantations were to have an enduring influence on the social and political life of Ulster. In their more immediate effect they introduced into the province an element of unrest that contributed materially to the insurrection of 1641. The Irish chiefs who had gone into exile or who had been subsequently dispossessed had maintained considerable personal bodyguards, 'swordsmen', for whom no provision was now made. Sir Arthur Chichester, the deputy, realised the danger and had some hundreds of them shipped off to Sweden to serve in the armies of Charles IX; but many more eluded capture and together with some of the dispossessed proprietors, who disdained to live as tenants on their former estates, they took shelter in the woods and hills, lived on the plunder of the countryside and kept alive the memory of the past until the time should come for striking another blow against the English power.

The Old English were not affected by the confiscations in Ulster. Their main grievance at the beginning of James's reign was religious, and their hope of improving their position was encouraged by the general ineffectiveness of the established church. The Elizabethan conquest had been accompanied by some efforts to carry out the acts of supremacy and uniformity. The Munster plantation, for example, had included plans for the establishment of protestant clergy in the parishes. But, despite this, contemporary accounts give a most gloomy picture of the state of affairs: the churches in ruins, ecclesiastical incomes turned to secular uses, the parochial clergy absentees or grossly incompetent, the bishops greedy pluralists, the people either abandoned to heathenism, with 'no more demonstration of religion than amongst Tartars or cannibals', or left to the ministration of the Roman catholic clergy, who, undeterred by danger and poverty, flocked into the country from continental seminaries. Even in the Pale there were often no churches for the people to attend, so that those who were willing to conform could not do so. While the reformed church showed so little sense of its responsibilities and made so little use of its advantages it was natural that the Roman catholics, fortified by their numbers and encouraged by the zeal of their clergy, should not rest satisfied with an ecclesiastical settlement which placed their enemies in possession of the machinery and endowments of the church. The accession of James I seemed to provide just such an opportunity as they had been waiting for. While king of Scotland he had been in communication with O'Neill and O'Donnell, he was supposed to be sympathetic towards his mother's faith and there was a general belief in Ireland that he would at least establish a legal toleration. Acting on these hopes the magistrates of Waterford, Kilkenny, Cork, Limerick and other of the southern towns seized the churches and handed them over to the Roman catholic clergy. Though some show of force on the part of the deputy soon restored order, the incident was a clear indication of the kind of problem which James would have to face. But in fact neither James nor Charles would ever face the problem squarely; they would neither enforce the law as it stood nor establish a legal toleration. Frequent but ineffective proclamations against the Roman catholics and occasional acts of severity prevented them from having any sense either of security or of gratitude; while the church of Ireland, though somewhat improved in discipline, could make little headway against their zealous and efficient clergy, whom the government seemed powerless to expel or control.

From the government's point of view the chief danger was that the religious sympathy between Irish and Old English would lead to political alliance. Since the reign of Elizabeth the common title of 'recusant' had been applied to all who refused the oath of supremacy, irrespective of their race; but divergent traditions of loyalty and difference of interest were still strong. The Old English recusants, unlike the native Irish, occupied a strong constitutional position, as appeared in the parliament which James called in 1613, partly to ratify the Ulster plantation, partly to secure some increase of revenue. The government had made careful preparations, including the creation of forty new boroughs, and when parliament met at Dublin in 1613 there was a considerable protestant majority. The recusants, who represented the wealth and property of the Old English, withdrew in protest, and the moral effect of this was so great that the govern-

ment dared not proceed in their absence. Parliament was pro-
rogued so that an inquiry could be made into their grievances;
many elections were disallowed and when it met again in October
1614 the protestant majority had been reduced to a very narrow
margin. As a result, the government had to abandon legislation
it had proposed against the Jesuits. But the other measures passed
by this parliament, including acts for the recognition of the king's
title and for the attainder of Tyrone and Tyrconnell, showed that
the secular loyalty of the recusants was still unimpaired. Nevertheless, the general outcome was unsatisfactory to the government. Not only had the recusants won a moral victory, but very
little had been done to increase the revenue, and in Ireland as in
England Stuart governments were perpetually short of money.
To remedy both these defects—to ensure an adequate protestant
majority in future parliaments and to increase the income of the
crown—James decided to push on more vigorously with the
policy of plantation.

In this new development the Old English suffered no less than
the native Irish and their common fear of dispossession brought
the two closer together. Thus the religious grievance, which was
already a potential bond of union between them, was now linked
with the question of land, for the colonists were protestants while
those on whose estates they settled were Roman catholics; this
concurrence of threats eventually drove the two races into a rather
uneasy alliance.

The basis of the new plantation policy was the revival of
dormant royal claims. In 1615 the crown lawyers began an attack
upon the titles of landlords in the county of Wexford and within
the next few years similar attacks were made in Longford, King's
County, Leitrim and elsewhere. It was an easy thing to find
flaws in the title to an Irish estate, and it was seldom difficult to
persuade or bully a jury into giving a verdict for the crown. There
was no intention of wholesale dispossession; where the king's
claim succeeded, a proportion of the land, usually one quarter,
was set aside for plantation, and the rest regranted to the former
occupant. This process certainly resulted in some pecuniary
profit to the crown, for a fine had to be paid for the new title and
a rent was reserved on the land. But the plantation part of the
scheme came to very little. Estates were granted to undertakers,
many of whom never visited the country, and who were in general
content to make what profit they could out of the existing holders.

This policy produced general uneasiness throughout the kingdom during the later years of James I. No one felt safe: even the new planters in Ulster were endangered through their failure to carry out strictly the terms of their undertakings. And there were other causes of grievance. James found the regular revenue, even when supplemented by income from plantation schemes, quite unequal to the cost of government; he was unwilling to risk another parliament, and in 1622 set up a court of wards, mainly for the sake of the financial profit. The use of the court as a means of proselytising, by entrusting the education of Roman catholic minors to protestant guardians, naturally aroused the hostility of the recusants.

The seriousness both of the unrest in the country and of the poverty of the government was increased by the break with Spain in 1624. It was obviously necessary to secure Ireland against a possible attack and to minimise the chance of a pro-Spanish insurrection. The general interests of England were so deeply involved in this that the English parliament voted a large sum for the defence of Ireland. The war with Spain was followed, early in the reign of Charles I, by war with France; the English parliament was not now so ready to assist the king, and it was therefore more than ever necessary that the revenue of Ireland should be increased. Out of these circumstances rose the idea of a bargain between the king and the Irish landlords, the king offering certain concessions in return for immediate financial help. After many months of discussion terms were agreed in May 1628: land-holders were not to be disturbed by royal claims based on titles more than sixty years old, and special guarantees were given for titles in Ulster and Connaught; the enforcement of the oath of supremacy was to be relaxed in certain cases; in return, the king was to have £120,000, paid over three years. It was intended that a parliament should meet to confirm these royal concessions (the 'Graces'), and the money paid in return for them was to be deducted from any subsidies granted by the parliament. In fact, however, the proposal to summon parliament was dropped; and the 'Graces', having no legal sanction, rested solely on the king's will.

Falkland, the deputy who had helped to negotiate the bargain of 1628, was recalled in the following year. He was an unpopular and not very successful ruler, but his immediate successors were a great deal worse. Charles did not at once appoint another deputy, but entrusted the government to two lords justices, Richard Boyle, earl of Cork, and Adam Loftus, the lord chancellor. Both were representatives of the new English interest established in Ireland during the reign of Elizabeth; they were able men, though greedy of gain, but their mutual hostility, apart from other difficulties, made efficient government impossible. In ecclesiastical affairs they were hampered by doubt about what the king really intended. Strict enforcement of the acts of uniformity and supremacy could not be expected, but protestant opinion in both kingdoms was alarmed at the open activity of the Jesuits and the establishment of religious houses, even in Dublin itself. Occasional attempts at suppression had no effect but to excite the anger of the recusants. To counter possible danger the lords justices had increased the army, but they had no money to pay it and the soldiers lived at free quarters on the country. The war with Spain had cut off one important part of Ireland's overseas trade, and the rest was seriously hampered by pirates, especially the Algerines, who were even strong enough to sack the port of Baltimore in 1630. Ireland seemed to be drifting into general confusion at the very time when Charles, who was now attempting to rule England without a parliament, was most in need of help. It was in these circumstances that the king decided to appoint as lord deputy Sir Thomas Wentworth, who had already rendered him good service as president of the council of the north. Wentworth arrived in Dublin in 1633 and from then until his final departure in 1640 he ruled Ireland sternly, in some respects unscrupulously, but on the whole more efficiently than she had ever been ruled before.

There was little in Wentworth's policy that was new, except the thoroughness with which he carried it out. By 1636 he had gone far towards reforming the worst abuses and disorders in church and state. Ecclesiastical lands and revenues had been recovered, churches rebuilt, clerical residence in some measure enforced, and convocation, though asserting its national independence, had been induced to accept the thirty-nine articles of the church of England. A parliament had been successfully held, and its generous grants had removed a burden of debt and helped to establish the revenue upon a firmer footing; and all this had been gained without any confirmation of the Graces. The coast had been cleared of pirates, trade was improving and the income from customs duties rising steadily. To Wentworth all this was a means to an end. His rule in Ireland must be considered in the light of his general policy; his great object was to break down throughout the British Isles every force which stood against the absolute authority of the crown and he was determined to use the resources of Ireland to strengthen the monarchy in Great Britain. For this reason he spent much of the increased revenue on the army. He paid it regularly, improved its discipline and saw that it was properly equipped. In 1639 he was prepared to use it to enforce the king's authority in Scotland, and the suspicion that he had also advised the king to use it in England added to the bitter zeal with which the English house of commons was later to insist upon his death.

The same subjection of Ireland to the main design appears in Wentworth's economic policy. The centre of royal power must always be in England and so Ireland must be kept in a dependent condition. He therefore discouraged the woollen industry, not only lest it should interfere with English prosperity, but also in order that Ireland might be forced to depend on England for supplies:

All wisdom advises to keep this kingdom as much subordinate and dependent on England as is possible; and holding them from the manufacture of wool, and thus enforcing them to fetch their clothing from thence . . . how can they depart from us without nakedness and beggary?

At the same time, he promoted the linen manufacture for which Ireland had formerly been famous, but which had declined during the Elizabethan wars, for this did not clash with any English interest.

When Wentworth left Ireland for the last time in April 1640 he declared that the Irish were 'as fully satisfied and as well affected to his majesty's person and service as can possibly be wished for'. This might have seemed true enough on the surface, but his government had done nothing to bring permanent tranquillity into Irish political life; and though it is false to regard Wentworth as mainly responsible for the insurrection of 1641 his policy undoubtedly contributed to the general unrest which showed itself soon after his departure. His refusal to confirm the Graces in parliament left the way open for a renewed attack upon land titles, which he pressed on with unscrupulous vigour. The court of Castle Chamber, the Irish equivalent of the English Star Chamber, was used to overawe juries which refused to find for the crown, and in this way lands were confiscated, fines exacted and rents imposed. The London companies in Ulster, the entire province of Connaught, Elizabethan settlers like the earl of Cork, all had to submit, and the ill-feeling aroused was more than enough to offset the effects of economic prosperity. The recusants enjoyed a great measure of toleration, but for this they had no security and were not likely to become reconciled to a position of permanent inferiority, while the failure to enforce the law against them alarmed and angered the protestants. Wentworth's ecclesiastical reforms, carried out largely under the influence of Laud, tended to alienate the more zealous of the clergy, for the Irish church was still very much affected by the calvinistic theology which was being gradually pushed out of the church of England. Thus almost every powerful interest in the kingdom, though forced into temporary submission, was ready to turn against Wentworth as soon as opportunity should offer. The merchants prospered; the common people were relieved from the burden of a rapacious soldiery and given some protection against brigands and pirates; in cases where crown interests were not concerned the courts administered justice with a strictness which Ireland had rarely known; but all this counted for little in a country dominated by landlords and torn by religious strife.

The situation in Ireland was closely affected by what was happening in Great Britain and this was particularly true of the north-east, which maintained a regular intercourse with Scotland. Here Wentworth's Laudian zeal had provoked another source of discord. The Scottish settlers in Ulster had brought their presbyterianism with them, but so far they had managed to live within the pale of the established church. Some of the northern bishops were Scots, and had allowed their countrymen to occupy livings without too strict an inquiry into their doctrine or any rigid insistence upon the acts of supremacy and uniformity. Such a state of affairs was a scandal to Laud and Wentworth. John Bramhall, a Yorkshireman who had come to Ireland as Wentworth's chaplain, was appointed to the see of Derry to enforce the discipline of the church. Under his leadership other bishops took similar action, and many ministers who refused to conform returned to Scotland, where they took a leading part in the agitation preceding the national covenant of 1638. But, though a

considerable degree of outward conformity was established in
Ulster, its insecurity was revealed in 1639. In that year, when war
threatened between England and Scotland, Wentworth tried to
ensure the loyalty of Ulster by imposing on the Scottish settlers an
oath of unconditional obedience to royal commands. The 'black
oath', as it was called, was refused by hundreds of people of all
ranks; some of them were seized and imprisoned, but great
numbers took refuge in the woods and hills, or fled back to
Scotland. Thus Wentworth not only added to his own enemies at
home and to the king's in Scotland, but he weakened and divided
the British and protestant interest in Ulster when it was on the
eve of a most dangerous assault.

2. INSURRECTION AND RECONQUEST, 1641-60

The outbreak and course of the Ulster insurrection of 1641 were
strongly influenced by the contemporary situation in Great
Britain, but its roots are to be found in the Elizabethan conquest
and in the plantations of the early seventeenth century. Some of
the native proprietors had been left in possession of all or part
of their lands, many of those who had been dispossessed remained
as tenants, others took to brigandage and gathered round them
considerable bodies of fighting men. Thus the memory of old
wrongs was kept alive and the nucleus of an army prepared
against the day of opportunity. Meanwhile, the numerous exiles
who had taken service with foreign powers kept in touch with their
countrymen and inspired them with hope of aid from abroad.
The successful resistance which the Scottish rebels had made to
royal authority in 1639 and 1640 was naturally an encouragement
to the malcontents in Ulster; and when the calling of the Long
Parliament led to the overthrow of Wentworth (now earl of
Strafford) and the consequent weakening of government in
Ireland they concluded that the time was ripe for action. Early in
1641 preparations began for an insurrection all over the kingdom,
beginning with the seizure of Dublin castle. The date fixed was
23 October; but at the last moment the plan was betrayed, the
castle was saved, and, though insurrection broke out on the
appointed day, it was at first confined to the north. Throughout
Ulster the natives rose against the colonists, massacred many
thousands of them and seized upon some of the most important
towns and strongholds; but the loyalists secured Londonderry,

Enniskillen and Carrickfergus, with other places of less note; and they kept control over important, though ill-defined, areas in the east and in the north-west. Elsewhere, however, the Irish forces, commanded by Sir Phelim O'Neill, dominated the province.

The fate of the insurrection hung upon the attitude of the Old English, and especially upon that of the Roman catholic lords and gentry of the Pale. Some of them undoubtedly had known of the conspiracy, but in general they were not actively involved. Their grievances were less acute than those of the Ulstermen, and their traditions inclined them to support the crown and to distrust the natives. Religion certainly formed a link with the latter; but for a long time they had enjoyed a practical toleration, and if this had seemed likely to continue they might have remained loyal or at least neutral. But the Long Parliament was showing itself aggressively protestant in Irish as well as in English affairs, and the lords justices who had taken over the government from Strafford were strongly puritan in sympathy. Stories of the Ulster massacres, horribly exaggerated, had aroused fury in London and panic in Dublin, and in both capitals the sternest measures were called for against all recusants, irrespective of race. In the circumstances, it was natural enough for the Old English to join with the rebels, and the greater part of them did so before the end of the year. The combined forces besieged Drogheda, a general invasion of the Pale began and the rising spread to Munster.

The horror and fear aroused in England by stories of the Irish rebellion might have been expected to produce speedy forces for its suppression. But the king had to depend on parliament for supply, and parliament, half suspecting that the king was himself in some way involved with the rebel leaders, was unwilling to trust him. The troops immediately available in Ireland were put under the command of the earl of Ormonde, head of the Butler family. He was a devoted royalist and there was little sympathy between him and the lords justices, who supported the puritan and parliamentary side in the contemporary quarrel in England. But in the first flush of disaster they were ready to turn anywhere for help, and Ormonde had a good reputation as a soldier. Under his direction the safety of Dublin was secured, and he was anxious to pass at once to the offensive before the rebels had time to organise themselves and collect arms. The lords justices, jealous of his authority, and fearful of weakening the defences of the capital, refused their consent. But by the end of

the year reinforcements at last began to arrive from England, and
in the spring Ormonde was allowed to advance on Drogheda which
he relieved in March. In the following month the protestant
position in Ulster was strengthened by the arrival of Major-
General Robert Monro with a Scottish force of 2,500 men.
Monro had learned his trade in the Thirty Years' War, his troops
were inflamed by tales of Irish atrocities, and the severities
practised during his first campaign in Down aroused the indignation of even such a hardened old soldier as Sir James Turner.
But he won considerable military success and established an
uneasy peace over a considerable part of Ulster.

The situation in Ireland was still further complicated by the
outbreak of the English civil war in August 1642. For the next
seven years, until the arrival of Cromwell in August 1649, the
'war of the three kingdoms' filled the country with the conflict
not only of armies but of diplomatists. There was no clear-cut
division of parties. The rebels, under the direction of the Roman
catholic bishops, set up a central government with its capital at
Kilkenny and summoned a 'general assembly for the kingdom of
Ireland', a kind of parliament representing the native and Old
English interests. They also appointed a Supreme Council to
carry on the war, and made provision for local government and
the administration of justice. But this 'Confederation of Kilkenny', though in arms against the government, professed loyalty
to the crown of England, and appealed to Magna Carta. The
native Irish and the Old English who had combined in this
confederation were held together mainly by their common
religion, and this bond was strengthened by the just conviction
that if the puritan party triumphed they would both suffer
equally. But whereas the Old English were uneasy at finding
themselves in rebellion and were ready to return to their allegiance
without insisting on religious concessions which the king might
find it dangerous to grant, the Irish, while not disowning their
duty to the crown, were more submissive to clerical direction and
were unwilling to accept less than their original demand that the
Roman catholic church should be fully re-established in Ireland.
Among the protestants there was the same sort of confusion. In
some measure all parties were held together by fear of the rebels;
but there were those who thought English rebels as dangerous to
royal authority as Irish, others who distrusted the king and

placed their reliance on parliament, others who cared for neither king nor parliament so long as the result turned to their own profit.

The attitude of every group was critically affected by the land question. Most of the native Irish had entered upon the war with little or no property; they were fighting to recover what they or their ancestors had lost, and as they risked little they were willing to stand out to the end. The Old English were, for the most part, possessed of estates; success might enrich them, but failure would be the ruin of themselves and their families, and they were ready for any reasonable settlement which would secure to them what they already had. On the protestant side, though there were a few native Irish, like Lord Inchiquin, and a few Old English, like Ormonde, the majority was made up of newly planted families, of government officials and of soldiers of fortune. Many of them looked forward to the defeat of the rebels as an opportunity of making money out of forfeited estates; they opposed a compromise settlement, and, provided the rebellion was suppressed, cared little whether by king or parliament. Even in England the Irish land question affected the course of politics, for parliament had raised great sums on the security of the prospective forfeitures, and the 'adventurers' who had advanced the money used their influence to push forward the policies most likely to bring them a profit.

In this confusion of religious and political and economic motives nothing could clarify the situation save decisive military success on one side or the other; but for a long time the war dragged on inconclusively. The confederates, though they had the advantage of numbers and controlled the greater part of the country, suffered from divided leadership. Owen Roe O'Neill, nephew of the great earl of Tyrone, commanded their forces in the north, and Thomas Preston, who belonged to a noble family of the Pale, commanded in Leinster. Both had served in the Spanish Netherlands, and a mutual jealousy there engendered made hearty co-operation between them impossible. The protestants also were divided—the Scots in the north, under Monro, the royalists of the Pale, under Ormonde, those of Munster, under Inchiquin—and the various groups gave each other little support; but they had rather the better of it in the desultory fighting of 1642 and 1643. During these years the protestant forces received some further help from England and Scotland,

but attention there was naturally concentrated on the struggle
between the king and parliament. The king's chief interest in
Ireland was to make a treaty with the rebels which would release
troops for service in England. Ormonde laboured hard at this
and concluded a 'cessation of arms' in September 1643. But there
was no real settlement, for Charles dared not grant terms which
would satisfy the confederation. In any case, Ormonde could
negotiate only for the forces under his direct command. The
Scots army in the north ignored the cessation and subscribed the
Solemn League and Covenant; the Munster protestants disowned Ormonde and adhered to the English parliament, which
had condemned the cessation without waiting to hear its terms.

Ormonde's difficulties were increased by the king's duplicity.
As the royal cause in England became more desperate, Charles's
scruples about concessions to the Irish recusants weakened. He
opened secret negotiations through the earl of Glamorgan, an
English Roman catholic, who made a treaty which the king was
obliged to repudiate as soon as it became public. But the Irish
and clerical party in the confederation, strengthened by the arrival
of a papal nuncio, Rinuccini, wished to reject Ormonde's more
moderate proposals and to insist upon the confirmation of the
Glamorgan treaty. For a time, however, the Old English dominated the Supreme Council and in March 1646 a new treaty was
made with Ormonde, secretly and without Rinuccini's knowledge.
Less than three months later, and before the treaty could take
effect, came the first great battle of the war, which temporarily
altered the balance of power in the confederation and put Rinuccini in control. On 5 June Owen Roe O'Neill and the Ulster
forces inflicted a crippling defeat on Monro at Benburb, seven
miles from Armagh. Monro's army was not wiped out, but he
lost all his artillery and a great quantity of arms, and for a time
he ceased to be dangerous. The military results of the victory were
surprisingly small, for O'Neill failed to follow it up. The political
results were more important; O'Neill's influence in the confederation was greatly strengthened, and with his support
Rinuccini was able to overthrow the Supreme Council, establish
himself in control and secure the repudiation of the Ormonde
peace. But the dissensions within the confederation could not so
easily be got rid of, and though Preston joined forces with
O'Neill for an attack upon Dublin their mutual distrust brought it
to nothing.

Though Dublin was saved for the time being, Ormonde's position had become almost impossible. He could not hold out much longer without help, and no help could be expected from the king, who had lost his last army and was now virtually a prisoner. Help might, indeed, be obtained from the English parliament, but only in return for submission to parliament's authority. Ormonde was thus in a dilemma, for he must surrender either to Irish or to English rebels. It was mainly in the hope that king and parliament might yet come to terms and save Ireland for the protestant faith and the English interest that he chose the latter course. On 18 June 1647 he handed over Dublin and the other garrisons that he still held to a parliamentary commander, and a month later sailed for England.

The complicated skein of negotiations which confused English and Scottish politics for the next two years naturally included Ireland also. When the royalist cause began to revive both Inchiquin and the Ulster Scots declared for the king. Ormonde returned and resumed his meetings with the confederates in the hope of building up a new royalist alliance. Owen Roe O'Neill, who still commanded a large army in the north, at first held aloof, then tried to come to terms with the parliamentary commanders on his own behalf and finally, when it was too late, promised to throw in his lot with Ormonde. But the time for negotiations had gone by and the future was to be decided by arms. In August 1649 Cromwell landed at Dublin with 12,000 men and a commission from parliament as lord lieutenant of Ireland.

Cromwell spent only nine months in Ireland and when he left in May 1650 the work of reconquest was still far from complete. But the vigour and cruelty of his campaigns and the ruthlessness of the settlement that he subsequently directed have left a mark and a memory that succeeding centuries have not been able to wipe out. He came to Ireland not only as a parliamentary commander pursuing the royalist enemy to his latest stronghold, but also as the avenger of blood, the minister (as he believed) of divine justice on those responsible for the cruelties which had been committed in the Ulster rising of 1641. It is this that explains not only the sack of Drogheda and of Wexford but even more the satisfaction that appears in Cromwell's reports. 'I am persuaded', he writes from Drogheda, after describing how 2,000 men were put to the sword, 'that this is a righteous judgement of God upon those barbarous wretches, who have imbrued their hands in so

much innocent blood.' It was in this spirit that the conquest of
Ireland was continued by Ireton and Ludlow; with the capitula-
tion of Galway in May 1652 the work was virtually completed.
By this time no central authority, royalist or confederate, was
left in the country to offer united opposition to the parliamentary
forces. Owen Roe O'Neill was dead. Rinuccini had gone home to
Italy, the confederation of Kilkenny was broken up, Ormonde
had joined Charles II in exile. Scattered garrisons and individual
commanders made what terms they could for themselves and
their troops, but the kingdom as a whole lay unconditionally at
the mercy of the victors.

The settlement of Ireland which followed this conquest was
dictated by both political and economic motives. In 1652 the
economic motive was the more urgent, for the claims against the
prospective forfeitures were mounting steadily. First came those
of the 'adventurers' who had advanced money under an act of
1642, the scope of which had been greatly enlarged by later
parliamentary ordinances. The arrears of pay due to the soldiers
and the debts due to the army contractors were also to be met
out of the fruits of the conquest. By 1653 the total of these claims
came to about three and a half million pounds. Besides all this,
the government hoped that there would be a surplus for general
purposes.

The political motive behind the settlement appeared in the
way in which it was carried out. By the Long Parliament's 'Act
for the settlement of Ireland', passed in 1652, every Irish proprietor who had resided in Ireland at any period during the war
and who could not prove his 'constant good affection to the
interests of the commonwealth of England' was to forfeit a proportion of his estate. By this sweeping measure almost every Irish
landlord, protestant and Roman catholic, native Irish or Old
English, royalist or confederate, was brought under condemnation. To clear the way for a thorough plantation, all the forfeiting
landlords were ordered to remove into Connaught or Clare, where
they were to receive an equivalent for the portion of their estates
to which they were entitled. In their place came a crowd of new
settlers, many of them officers in the commonwealth armies. This
transportation affected only the landlords and some of their more
substantial tenants; the bulk of the population, tradesmen,
farmers, and labourers, remained behind: it was a change of

proprietors, not of population. But its effect was to alter decisively the balance of political power. In 1641 the majority of Irish land-lords were Roman catholics; after the Cromwellian settlement the majority were protestants, and the commonwealth government looked upon them as the best guarantee for the maintenance of English authority in Ireland. The same aggressive nationalism can be seen in the measures against the Roman catholics, especially in the attempt to exclude them from cities and boroughs; for though there was a good deal of religious animosity, there was also a basic conviction that Roman catholics could never be loyal to the English interest.

The long-drawn-out struggle of these years had a disastrous effect on the economic life of the country. The prosperity built up under Wentworth disappeared. Trade was almost at a stand-still; land fell out of cultivation; war, famine and disease seriously reduced the population. Even when the actual fighting was over there was no immediate improvement. Uncertainty about owner-ship discouraged the careful development of estates, and the population was further reduced by emigration. Some thirty or forty thousand soldiers of the disbanded Irish armies, encouraged by the commonwealth government, took service abroad, most of them with Spain; and there was also a systematic policy of transporting 'vagrants' to the West Indies as indentured servants. On the other hand, many of the new settlers were able and enter-prising men, and the economic recovery which was a feature of the later seventeenth century had begun before the restoration of Charles II.

The social changes brought about by the Cromwellian con-quest and settlement were lasting. The constitutional changes were drastic but short-lived. In 1641 Ireland had a parliament of her own, shackled by Poynings' law and subject to English direction, but still able in some measure to represent and defend Irish interests. Under the commonwealth this was swept away and Ireland, like Scotland, was given representation in a central parliament, which legislated for the whole British Isles. In the confusion that followed the death of Oliver Cromwell and the collapse of the protectorate this parliamentary union broke up. A convention representing the parliamentary constituencies, which met in Dublin in February 1660, asserted the right of Ireland to a distinct legislature, while at the same time repudiating any idea of separating Ireland from England. Such an assertion of national

independence might seem to come strangely from the Cromwellian settlers who dominated the convention; but their main
loyalty was to their newly-won estates, and this seemed at the
time the best means of safeguarding them. The same selfish interest
led them to accept the restoration of monarchy. By this time it
was a strong possibility, and some of the more far-seeing members
of the convention were already in touch with the king. There was
no explicit bargain, but Charles made it clear that he would
respect the existing land settlement; thus reassured, the convention was ready to declare in his favour. It was, however, part
of the royal policy that England should appear to lead the way;
so the king's friends in Ireland held back, and he was not proclaimed in Dublin until 14 May, six days after his proclamation
in London. But the attitude of the Irish Cromwellians had
strengthened his hand during a critical period and he realised
how important it was to retain their support.

3. FROM RESTORATION TO REVOLUTION

For Ireland the period between the restoration and the revolution
was one of prolonged crisis. On the surface, there was some
appearance of tranquillity. The country became more prosperous; revenue increased; despite local disturbances the authority
of government was maintained; Ireland was more peaceful than
Scotland during the covenanting wars, and calmer than England
during the 'popish plot' scare. But there was no sense of security,
for the twin problems of land and religion, which had received a
violent solution under Cromwell, were naturally revived at the
restoration. This revival brought little immediate benefit to the
Roman catholic gentry, for they recovered only a small fraction
of their former estates, but they were not left without hope of
doing better; while this hope remained the protestants in possession could not feel safe. The struggle between the parties
came to the surface in the revolutionary war, but it had never
been really abandoned during the interval.

The restoration land settlement failed because it was impossible to satisfy all the conflicting claims. The Cromwellian
settlers had taken a leading part in restoring royal authority and
Charles had bound himself to respect their rights. But other
groups also had to be considered. There were consistent royalists

who must be restored without delay. There were occasional
royalists, who had found themselves fighting for the king at some
stage of the complicated warfare of the previous twenty years and
now hoped to recover what they had lost under the commonwealth. There were former rebels who claimed to be restored
under one or other of the treaties made with the confederation of
Kilkenny. There were royalist officers claiming arrears of pay.
There were those who had served Charles abroad, even if they
had fought against his father at home, and who now flocked
back in the hope of recovering something out of the general
confusion.

The Cromwellians had the great advantage of being in possession, and powerful forces in England were financially interested
in keeping them there. The agents of the Irish convention assured
Charles that there was in fact enough land to satisfy everyone,
and on the strength of this assurance he issued, in November
1660, a declaration promising to preserve the existing settlement
and at the same time to ensure that no one deserving restoration
should suffer. Ormonde's comment on this sums up its unreality: 'There must be new discoveries of a new Ireland, for the
old will not serve to satisfy these engagements.' However, a
parliament was summoned to turn this declaration into an act.
Here again the Cromwellians had an advantage, for being in
possession they practically controlled the elections, and the new
house of commons was almost completely in their hands. Something of its character can be seen in the fact that it was entirely
protestant; the recusant opposition of earlier parliaments had
been eliminated.

If it had had a completely free hand this parliament would
simply have confirmed the existing state of affairs; but the
operation of Poynings' law gave other interests some chance of
being considered. The details of the settlement were worked out
in England and the agents of the various parties concerned were
allowed to present their claims. The compromise finally reached in
the 'act of explanation' (1665)[1] was heavily weighted in favour of
the Cromwellians, but it did compel them to surrender something. They were to give up one-third of their holdings, and this
land, with other lands confiscated by the commonwealth government but not distributed, was to form a sort of fund from which

1. Its purpose was to 'explain' an 'act of settlement' (1662), which had confirmed the royal declaration of November 1660, and had proved unworkable.

various claims could be met. It was far from sufficient for the
purpose, and even claimants whose restoration was specifically
provided for in the act of explanation were not always able to
recover their estates.

In the long run, a considerable amount of land was restored to
those who had held it in 1641, or to their heirs. But there was
little order or justice in the restoration and court favour usually
counted for more than merit. The many former proprietors who
remained unsatisfied, most of them Roman catholics, did not at
once give up hope or tamely submit to their fate. Those whose
means or influence enabled them to engage in politics frequented
the court and sought allies for a general attack upon the whole
settlement. Others, as after the Ulster plantation, remained at
home and took to brigandage. Thus the restoration land system
was subjected to constant attack. Landlords of the Cromwellian
(or 'New English') interest saw with alarm the favour shown by
Charles II to Roman catholic adventurers like Richard Talbot;
and the prevalence of 'tories'[1] was a constant reminder of the
possibility of another 'forty-one'. In the circumstances, few
proprietors felt that their title-deeds, though guaranteed by act
of parliament, were safe from all danger of being questioned.

The bulk of the old protestant landlords, whose claims went
back beyond 1641, had either supported parliament and so held
on to their estates under the commonwealth, or else, as consistent
royalists, had recovered their losses shortly after the restoration.
So the protestant interest in Ireland, both old and new, was
substantially satisfied, while the Roman catholics, or a great
proportion of them, were in favour of a general upheaval.
Naturally, then, protestant opinion was alarmed at the toleration
with which Charles seemed determined to treat the latter. Their
clergy, secular and regular, moved freely about the country;
schools and convents were established; episcopal synods were held
with at least the tacit approval of the government. There was, of
course, no formal security in this toleration by connivance, as
was shown during the 'popish plot' scare; but the general character
of the period can be seen from the fact that the Irish commanders
at Limerick in 1691, anxious to get the best terms they could,
stipulated that 'the Roman catholics of this kingdom shall enjoy

---

1. Gaelic *toiridhe*, 'a pursuer', hence 'a robber'. The English form of the word,
in the sense of 'brigand' or 'outlaw', appears in the state papers at least as early as
the 1650s.

such privileges in the exercise of their religion . . . as they did enjoy in the reign of King Charles II'.

The alarm aroused among protestants by this policy of toleration extended to England, where Irish affairs exercised great influence in the party politics of the period. The king, if he chose to press on with his 'catholic design', could count on a great body of support in Ireland, not merely on religious grounds, but because the dispossessed Irish proprietors hoped that he would help them to recover their estates. For the same reason, the opposition looked jealously upon Ireland as a potential weapon in the king's hand for the overthrow of protestantism and parliamentary government in England. Some of the bitterest debates in the English parliament turned upon royal policy in Ireland; and the general hatred and fear of 'Irish papists', sedulously fostered by the whigs, was an important factor in the overthrow of the Stuart monarchy.

The question of religious toleration was complicated by the clear emergence of protestant dissent. The various sects introduced into Ireland during the commonwealth period disappeared soon after the restoration, and only the quakers survived into the eighteenth century as a distinct body. But the Scots presbyterians long established in Ulster were in a different position. After living uneasily for over thirty years within the pale of the established church, they had, in the 1640s, set up their own ecclesiastical system, and by the time of the restoration were organised throughout Ulster on the presbyterian model. Naturally enough, they opposed the re-establishment of episcopacy, and when they failed to prevent it were not inclined to submit. Under the commonwealth, many of their ministers had got possession of livings, especially in the counties of Antrim and Down, and they saw no reason why they should surrender them. The Irish bishops, however, without waiting for parliament to meet, resolved to enforce the law, and expelled all incumbents who had not been episcopally ordained: Jeremy Taylor, whose dioceses of Down and Connor and Dromore covered the chief area of presbyterian power, declared thirty-six parishes vacant in one day. But beyond this there was at first little actual persecution and the expelled ministers continued to live and work among their congregations.

The situation was changed by the outbreak of an abortive insurrection in 1663, for though this was mainly the work of

Cromwellian 'fanatics' a few presbyterians were involved. Some ministers were imprisoned and others forced to leave the kingdom. But even then there was no regular or sustained effort to enforce uniformity, and in a few years things began to return to their former state; ministers came back to their congregations and meeting-houses were built to take the place of the parish churches which they had been compelled to restore. In 1672 Charles II began the payment, not very regularly maintained, of an annual grant of £600 to be distributed among the presbyterian ministers of Ulster. But this *regium donum* was not so much a mark of favour as a precautionary bribe, and until after the revolution the Irish government kept an anxious watch on the northern presbyterians and their frequent contacts with Scotland.

The firm assertion of episcopal authority against protestant dissenters was typical of the restored church of Ireland, which now entered upon a period of vigorous life. Convocation met once more, and, without waiting for the approval of parliament, adopted and enforced the English prayer book of 1662. The right of the clergy to tax themselves was recognised. Trinity College, Dublin, where most of the Irish clergy were educated, was reformed by Jeremy Taylor, as vice-chancellor. In the 1680s the complete Bible was at last published in Irish, but did less than its promoters had expected towards converting the 'popish natives'. The church still suffered from many abuses, but the standard of piety and learning was probably higher than it had been for centuries. The learning of churchmen was not narrowly confined, and clergy formed a high proportion of the membership of the Dublin Philosophical Society, the Irish equivalent of the Royal Society in England. But though the church was in some respects stronger than before the civil war it had become clearer than ever that it was not the church of the people. From the restoration onwards, religious life in Ireland flowed in the three well-marked streams of Anglicanism, Roman catholicism and protestant dissent.

In spite of the instability produced by the half-solved problems of land and religion, the economic recovery which had begun under the commonwealth continued more rapidly after the restoration. This prosperity rested very largely upon the raising of cattle, which many factors combined to make the country's chief industry: the soil was particularly suitable; labour was scarce; few of the landlords had much capital, and those who

had were unwilling to risk it in the development of estates which
they were under constant fear of losing. In the early 1660s these
cattle formed Ireland's most valuable export, and tens of thousands of them were sent annually to England, where they were
fattened for the market on the rich western pastures. But this
thriving trade roused the jealousy of the English parliament, and
acts of 1663 and 1666 excluded Irish cattle completely from
England. In fact, this exclusion did Ireland little harm, for Irish
merchants soon turned their attention to the continent and found
a profitable market for their beef and other cattle products in
Flanders, France, Spain and Portugal. But the cattle acts are
important as indications of a new English policy towards Irish
trade, a policy of hampering the prosperity of Ireland in the
interests of England. This appears in other measures of Charles II's
reign, especially in the restriction of Irish trade with the American
plantations and in the restraint placed upon the export of Irish
wool to the continent. Though these restrictions were significant
for the future, Ireland did not suffer much from them at the time.
A steady rise in customs revenue and an increase in the value of
land indicate clearly that the country was becoming more prosperous. But this prosperity rested on a narrow basis, and attempts
to make it more secure by the encouragement of textile manufactures had, at this time, little success.

Ireland's economic position was also weakened by the drain
of money to England. Though absentee landlords were not as
numerous as they became in the eighteenth century, they drew a
considerable sum in rents out of the kingdom, and the increasing
surplus revenue also went to England. This surplus was entirely
in the king's hand, for the Irish parliament had deprived itself of
any effective control by the very generous settlement which it
made at the restoration. The old hereditary revenue, as it existed
when parliament met in 1661, brought in about £40,000 a year.
Parliament made several very important additions,[1] and the
annual income from both old and new revenue was expected to be
£240,000. As trade improved this sum was considerably exceeded
and in 1678 the Irish revenues were farmed out at £300,000 a
year. The total cost of the civil and military establishments was
estimated at less than £200,000 a year, so that there should have
been a very considerable surplus. In fact, as a result of peculation
and mismanagement, the army was usually short of equipment

1. Including a hearth-tax which was particularly burdensome on the poor.

and in arrears of pay; but the king and his friends were able to draw large sums out of the Irish revenue, and these of course were spent in England. The financial settlement of the restoration made the government independent of parliamentary supply; so in 1666, when parliament had dealt with land and revenue and other outstanding questions, it was dissolved, and was not summoned again until the reign of James II.

The heaviest call upon the Irish revenue was the maintenance of the armed forces. Apart from the militia, these amounted in 1666 to about 1,600 horse and 5,000 foot; their maintenance cost £168,000, or seventy per cent of the estimated revenue. This was a large and expensive army for Ireland to keep up; but it was not merely a defence force against possible invasion, it was also an instrument of government; the troops were distributed over the country in small garrisons and almost constantly engaged in the work of suppressing tories. They were ill-paid, often inefficient and sometimes mutinous, but it is hard to see how the administration could have been carried on without them. Though the Irish army was thus required in Ireland, the king was anxious to use it elsewhere; a standing army maintained out of hereditary revenue, and consequently free from parliamentary inquiry, was a source of strength which he was not likely to overlook. Charles was more cautious than either his father or his brother and did not propose to bring Irish troops into England. But in 1674 and again in 1679 an Irish force was prepared for service in Scotland, to help in suppressing the covenanters, and though it was never sent its readiness to act was of considerable value to the Scottish government. The Irish army also provided part of the garrison of Tangier. This was of double advantage to the king, for it not only saved English money but it enabled him to keep at home English troops whom he was very unwilling to send abroad.

Though the English parliament could not object to this use of Irish resources to serve the general interests of the monarchy, it did watch royal policy in Ireland with suspicion. The king had much more freedom of action in Irish than in English affairs, and parliament feared that he might use that freedom to build up financial and military resources with which to overthrow parliamentary government in England. These fears were not entirely groundless. There can be no doubt that Ireland was intended to play an important part in the 'catholic design', and during the cabal ministry great favour was shown to Irish Roman catholics, and they were even given some reason to hope that the land settlement would be modified in their favour. All this drew a strong protest from the English house of commons, the king was compelled to follow a more cautious course, and royal policy received a fresh check in the outbreak of the 'popish plot' scare in 1678.

The political agitators who busily turned Oates's revelations to party advantage could not ignore Ireland, for it was inevitable that the strong Roman catholic interest there would be concerned in any 'popish plot'. They professed to uncover a conspiracy for the murder of Ormonde, at that time lord lieutenant, and he was accordingly instructed to disarm the Roman catholics, strengthen the garrisons and generally put the kingdom in a state of defence. But Ormonde refused to be frightened. He took such precautions as he considered wise, and laboured hard to persuade the protestants that any sign of panic would be a great encouragement to their enemies. Under his confident guidance the country remained calm. But the policy of practical toleration was interrupted, and Ireland supplied one of the most illustrious victims of the public frenzy, Archbishop Oliver Plunket of Armagh, a man of peaceful life and genuine loyalty. He was among the last to suffer for the 'plot', and in the royalist reaction which soon followed the Irish Roman catholics recovered their former freedom.

This royalist reaction, and the financial assistance of Louis XIV, enabled Charles to free himself from parliamentary control, and during the last years of his reign he moved steadily towards the establishment of an absolute and Roman catholic monarchy. But before Ireland could play its full share in this plan the government there would have to be recast by the admission of Roman catholics to both civil and military positions. Such a sweeping change could hardly be carried through while Ormonde was lord lieutenant, for, though opposed to persecution, he was a strong churchman, and would never be a willing instrument in a plot to overthrow the protestant constitution of the three kingdoms. Charles therefore decided to remove him, but died before his purpose was fulfilled, and Ormonde remained in office long enough to proclaim James II. Almost immediately afterwards he left Ireland for the last time.

The event deserves a moment's retrospect, for Ormonde was the dominant figure of restoration Ireland. He was lord lieutenant from 1661 to 1669 and again from 1677 to 1685, and even when he was out of office his influence was considerable. A man of ancient family and great estate, lord high steward of England, chancellor of the university of Oxford, the friend of Clarendon and one of the acknowledged leaders of the old cavalier party, he was, apart altogether from the lord lieutenancy, one of the greatest subjects of the crown. The source of his influence lay not only in these accidents of birth and breeding, but also in his own character. His parts were solid rather than brilliant. He was industrious and reliable, a shrewd judge of men and events, and above all he had a clear honesty of purpose, based on a strong though unostentatious piety. His removal from office was a turning point in the history of the British Isles, for it marked the first important step towards that breach in the old alliance of church and crown which was to prove fatal to James II.

The death of Charles and the departure of Ormonde produced anxiety among Irish protestants; as the new sovereign's policy revealed itself this anxiety turned to consternation. The struggle which reached its climax at the Boyne and ended at Limerick ran a clear course from the accession of James II. The events of these years showed how completely religious and political divisions had become identified in Ireland. Once the fighting began, even protestants who professed loyalty to James were disarmed and imprisoned. At the same time, Anglicans and presbyterians sank their differences in face of a common danger. The former distinctions between 'native Irish' and 'Old English' finally disappeared, and 'Irish' and 'Roman catholic' became almost interchangeable terms. But the Gaelic aristocracy and its traditions had gone for ever; the Irish of the revolutionary wars were led mainly by men of English descent.

James knew that Englishmen were deeply interested in the maintenance of protestant supremacy in Ireland; but he wanted the help of the Irish and it was only to be secured by giving them control of the government. The agent he chose for the purpose was one little likely to reassure protestant opinion. Colonel Richard Talbot was the brother of the Roman catholic archbishop of Dublin; during the reign of Charles II he had engaged in various schemes for the overthrow of the restoration land settlement, and the English house of commons had urged the king to remove him from court. He was a brave man, but unreliable and something of a braggart, not greatly respected

Modern Ireland

even among his own party. In 1685 James made him earl of
Tyrconnell and sent him to Ireland to carry out the new policy.
Within a short time the army was purged of protestants; Roman
catholics were appointed as judges and admitted to the privy
council; the municipal corporations were remodelled so as to
secure Roman catholic majorities. In Tyrconnell's mind the
crown of this work was to be a parliament in which the acts of
settlement and explanation would be repealed and the old
proprietors restored to their estates. While James remained on
the English throne he was not likely to consent to a measure
which would destroy one of the main guarantees of English
power in Ireland; but the English revolution and James's flight
to France in December 1688 altered the situation. Ireland had
contributed substantially to James's overthrow, for thousands
of Irish protestants, alarmed at Tyrconnell's policy, had flocked
over to England where they added to the general discontent and
alarm; and James's calling in of Irish troops had done more than
anything else to turn public opinion against him.

Events in England did not at once affect Tyrconnell's power.
He continued to rule in James's name and the greater part of
Ireland still acknowledged his authority. The one centre of
resistance was in the north, where the protestants were strong in
numbers as well as in property, and here William and Mary were
proclaimed king and queen in March 1689. But the protestant
forces were not well organised and after one brief encounter in
the field they were glad to take refuge behind the walls of Enniskillen and Londonderry.

This was the position when James himself landed at Kinsale
in March 1689. His main aim was to use Ireland as a base for
the recovery of England; but he was now so completely in the
hands of the Irish that the settlement of their claims could no
longer be delayed. In May a parliament met in Dublin.[1] The
measures taken by Tyrconnell against the corporations, the
flight of so many protestants, and the state of affairs in Ulster
combined to produce a house of commons which was almost
exclusively Roman catholic and a house of lords which was
predominantly so. This assembly carried through a social and
political revolution with which James had little sympathy, for

1. This parliament was subsequently declared invalid. Apart from the question
of James's legal title at the time, the procedure required by Poynings' law was not
followed, for obvious reasons.

he was still an English king and so bound to support the English interest in Ireland. He resisted successfully a demand for the repeal of Poynings' law; but he could not prevent the passage of a 'declaratory act' denying the right of the English parliament to bind Ireland and forbidding appeals from Irish courts to the English house of lords. It was this act especially which earned for this parliament the title of the 'patriot parliament'. Other measures established formal liberty of conscience and largely disendowed the church of Ireland. But the great work of the 'patriot parliament' was the making of a new land settlement. This was accomplished by two acts. The first repealed the acts of settlement and explanation and so restored the legal situation to what it had been before the insurrection of 1641. The second was an act of attainder, of which the practical effect was to confiscate the estates of over 2,000 protestant landlords. James opposed the latter, because he knew how disastrous it would be to his interests in England; but parliament forced it through and took the precaution of limiting the royal right of pardon. This new land settlement, despite all that has been said against it, was neither more nor less just than the Cromwellian and restoration settlements which it reversed. Like them, it was really an act of war; and people who are struggling, or believe they are struggling, for life, land, liberty and religion usually look to the end rather than to the means, and seldom worry about nice points of legality or justice.

While the Irish parliament was thus dividing the spoil the task of securing it was going forward but slowly. In April, James marched north to restore his authority in Ulster, and after some delay concentrated his forces against Londonderry, the chief centre of resistance. The city was closely besieged for fifteen weeks, but in spite of great privation held out until the arrival of an English squadron with supplies and reinforcements obliged the besiegers to retire. The interval thus gained was of great importance to William, for it enabled him to prepare an expeditionary force in England. This reached Ulster in August 1689 and kept the way open until William himself arrived, in June 1690, with a large and efficient army. In the meantime, James had received a reinforcement of 7,000 troops from France. On 1 July the two armies met on the river Boyne, some three miles above Drogheda, and James was decisively beaten. The battle was of

great importance to England and France as well as to Ireland.
Had it not been balanced by the French naval victory off Beachy
Head on the previous day Louis XIV might have been obliged
to make peace at once. As it was, William's position in England
was made secure; and though the war in Ireland dragged on for
over a year, James himself recognised the final nature of his
defeat by leaving the country almost immediately. But the battle
had a purely Irish as well as an international significance. The
instinct which has kept its memory alive in Irish politics is a true
one, for the Boyne was the critical moment of a long struggle
between the Roman catholic and protestant interests. The fact
that the protestants were allied with England and led by a Dutch
prince, while the Roman catholics were allied with France and
led by an English king, might complicate the situation but could
not alter its essential character. The 'protestant nation' which was
to dominate Ireland in the eighteenth century here established its
supremacy; and Irish protestants, even when engaged in a bitter
struggle for emancipation from English control, never ceased to
honour the 'glorious and immortal memory' of William III.

After the Boyne William occupied Dublin without resistance,
and there the war should have ended. The Irish had given up
hope of victory and fought on only for reasonable terms, which
William, anxious for a quick settlement, was quite ready to grant.
He proposed to offer a general guarantee of life and lands to all
who submitted; but (says Bishop Burnet) 'the English in Ireland
opposed this. They thought the present opportunity was not to be
let go of breaking the great Irish families'. A proclamation which
promised merely life and personal estate produced no effect, and
the war continued until the last Irish force surrendered at Limerick
in October 1691. Sarsfield, the Irish hero of the revolutionary
war, had defended the city gallantly while any hope of effective
aid from France remained, and in the end he was able to secure
fairly good terms, embodied in the famous treaty of Limerick.
The military articles of the treaty provided for the transport to
the continent of those Irish soldiers who wished to take service
abroad. The civil articles contained a general promise that the
Roman catholics should have the same degree of toleration as in
the reign of Charles II, and there were particular stipulations for
the estates and other interests of gentlemen then in arms and those
under their protection. On these terms Limerick was surrendered,

and thousands of Irish troops went abroad, the beginning of that
'flight of the wild geese' which was to draw off from Ireland
almost all that was best among the remaining gentry of Gaelic
and Old English blood. The military articles were carried out on
the spot; the civil articles required parliamentary confirmation
which the king had promised to make every effort to secure. But
the Irish parliament proved obstinate, William had to give way
on many points, and when at length the articles were confirmed
in 1697 it was in a form which conferred little advantage on those
whom they were intended to benefit.

4

THE PROTESTANT NATION, 1691–1800

I. IRELAND AFTER THE REVOLUTION

The end of the revolutionary war reproduced in some measure the conditions of 1603. Another conquest had been completed and once more Ireland lay helpless before the conqueror. But behind this similarity there was an essential difference, arising from the confiscations and plantations which had taken place in the interval. In 1603 the whole of Ireland was for the first time brought under effective English control and what was virtually a new administrative and legislative system had to be built up; in 1691 there was an administrative and legislative system already in existence and there was a loyal population ready to work it. Ireland had been reconquered not only for the crown but also for the 'English in Ireland'. These were for the most part descended from the settlers of the Tudor and Stuart periods, though they included also a few of the Old English and native Irish; their distinguishing mark was not their racial origin but their protestantism. The 'protestant ascendancy' thus established lasted throughout the eighteenth century and was only gradually broken down in the nineteenth.

The ascendancy was in origin and purpose a colonial garrison. But though difference of religion prevented its absorption by the Roman catholic majority and though it never ceased, in some ways, to be English, it rapidly developed a spirit of independence. The more secure it felt at home the more bitterly did it resent the restrictions placed by England upon its parliament and its trade, and the more strongly did it assert the national claims of Ireland.

In an age when political power was almost inseparably linked with property there was nothing incongruous in the protestant minority regarding themselves as the Irish people. Sir Jonah Barrington could even deduce their rights from the independent status of the Irish kings of pre-Norman times.[1] Thus there grew up in eighteenth-century Ireland a new nationalism, which owed little or nothing to the tradition of Hugh O'Neill, the confederation of Kilkenny and Patrick Sarsfield; which commemorated the battle of the Boyne and stood fast by the protestant succession; but which also was determined to secure its own rights against English intervention.

There was a fatal weakness in this protestant nationalism. It could never ally itself wholeheartedly with the mass of the people, for the religious barrier was too strong; and it could not push its quarrel with England beyond a certain point, for its own supremacy depended upon military force, which, in the last resort, it might have to call upon England to supply. Herein lay the dilemma of the Irish protestant—the dilemma which had faced Ormonde in 1647 when he surrendered Dublin to the parliamentary commander rather than to the confederate forces, and which was to face the Irish parliament at the end of the eighteenth century when it accepted a legislative union with England as a safeguard against the violent overthrow of the existing social and political order.

Such problems of choice did not arise in the period immediately following the revolution. At that point the task before the Irish protestants was a straightforward one. They had just escaped complete destruction, the sense of danger was still acute and they were determined, above all else, to secure their position for the future. In doing this they found occasion to assert their right of managing their own affairs in their own way. The confiscations which followed the war had reduced the lands held by Roman catholics to about one-fifteenth of the area of the whole kingdom. But the protestants were still jealous of their political power and anxious to curb it. For this reason they criticised bitterly the tolerant spirit of William's administration. When the Irish parliament met in 1692 it asserted its exclusively protestant character by tendering to every member of both houses an oath

1. Sir Jonah Barrington was a near contemporary of Grattan. His *Rise and fall of the Irish nation* (1833) is a history of the Irish parliament in the latter part of the eighteenth century.

D

denying the papal power to depose sovereigns and a declaration
against transubstantiation, and it refused to confirm the civil
articles of the treaty of Limerick, which William, in accordance
with his promise, placed before it. Another parliament, later in
the reign, did confirm the articles, though in a mutilated form;
but in defiance of the whole spirit of the treaty and against the
king's wishes it also initiated a series of penal enactments against
Roman catholics, which, with additions from time to time,
continued to be at least nominally in force until almost the end
of the eighteenth century.

These penal laws have been compared with the almost contemporary French laws against the Huguenots, upon which
they may have been partly based; but the circumstances in which
they were enacted and the ends which they served were very
different. They were directed against the religion of the great
bulk of the population, not against that of a tiny minority;
they arose from political fear, not from missionary zeal or an
authoritarian desire for uniformity; their general purpose was
degradation rather than conversion. The Irish penal code, unlike
the French, cannot be regarded as religious persecution, in the
strict sense of the term, for there was no effort to suppress Roman
catholic worship. An act of 1703 provided for the registration of
'popish priests', and though laws were passed for the expulsion
of dignitaries and of regular clergy, they were not enforced. But
while their worship was to be tolerated the Roman catholics
themselves were to be deprived of all political influence. They
were excluded not only from parliament but also from the army
and the militia, from every branch of the civil service, from
municipal corporations and from the legal profession. They were
forbidden to send their children abroad to be educated, and
efforts were made to keep all education at home under the control
of the established church.

All these restrictions bore most heavily upon the gentry, and it
was against them that the penal code was really directed. The
peasantry were not regarded as dangerous, but the few surviving
Roman catholic proprietors were. For this reason parliament
was above all determined that land, the key to political power,
should not pass into their hands. They were forbidden to acquire
it from a protestant by purchase, inheritance or gift, nor might
they lease it for a longer term than thirty-one years. A Roman
catholic proprietor had no power to leave land at will. On his

death it was to be divided among his sons, but if the eldest became a protestant he was to inherit all. If his conversion took place during his father's life-time the latter became merely a life-tenant, without power to alienate any part of the estate. If a protestant woman, owning land, married a Roman catholic her land passed at once to the protestant next-of-kin; if a Roman catholic wife turned protestant all her real property was released from her husband's control. Thus the amount of land held by Roman catholic proprietors could not increase and was almost bound to diminish.

The whole of this penal system was not and could not be rigidly enforced. Children were frequently sent abroad to be educated, and schools were established at home. Bishops and regular clergy moved about the country with some inconvenience, but little danger. Even the land laws could be evaded, and some Roman catholic families retained their estates entire throughout the whole penal period, usually by the co-operation of friendly protestants. But in its general purpose the system was successful. The Roman catholic majority soon ceased to be dangerous; the Jacobite insurrections of 1715 and 1745 produced no disturbance in Ireland; and until the land purchase schemes of the nineteenth century the bulk of the land remained in protestant ownership. The very success of the penal laws had an unforeseen result. The ablest and most active among the Roman catholic gentry took service abroad, those who remained at home were excluded from public life, and so, in the absence of an intelligent professional middle class to take their place, political leadership passed naturally to the clergy. The great political power of the Roman catholic church in modern Ireland can be traced directly to the effectiveness of the eighteenth-century penal code.

The Irish parliament was equally determined to have its own way in dealing with the protestant dissenters. It rejected William III's proposal for a toleration act, complained bitterly about the payment of *regium donum*, which he had renewed and increased, and even brought about its temporary suspension at the end of Anne's reign. In Anne's reign, also, a sacramental test was imposed. This excluded protestant dissenters, as well as Roman catholics, from the public service and, what was of far more importance to them, from municipal corporations. Though parliament did not take the initiative in the matter, it accepted the test, and steadily resisted all the efforts of English whig governments to have it repealed.

This policy of exclusiveness was frequently condemned, both by the dissenters themselves and by their whig allies in England, as ungrateful and impolitic. The part played by the presbyterians in resisting James II, and the apparent need for uniting the whole protestant interest of Ireland against the Roman catholic majority, might seem to give weight to this condemnation. But it is not hard to see the motives that influenced the churchmen. The presbyterians of Ulster, though they did not include many landlords, were strong in numbers and organisation, and in many areas they had established a virtual monopoly of trade. They made no effort to conceal their hostility to the episcopal system and their frequent contacts with Scotland kept ever before them an example of presbyterian triumph. Bishops and landlords naturally looked with anxiety upon such a strong and hostile body, and thought more of present rivalry than of former alliance. Besides this, they were convinced, and with reason, that if any danger of Roman catholic domination should recur the presbyterians would be bound to throw in their lot once more with the established church and, for their own sakes, support the revolution settlement to the end, even if they considered it in some respects unfair to themselves.

As the century progressed both sides became more tolerant. The effect of the sacramental test was mitigated by a series of indemnity acts, and the test itself, so far as it affected protestant dissenters, was finally removed in 1780. But by this time there was a new factor in the situation. The fear of political domination by the Roman catholics had greatly declined, and the more liberal-minded among the presbyterians were ready to accept them as allies against the whole system of privilege on which the protestant ascendancy was built. This alliance, incomplete though it was, helped to produce the revolutionary turmoil in which the parliamentary independence of Ireland was destroyed.

The degradation of the Roman catholics and the exclusion of the protestant dissenters from public life strengthened the political position of the church of Ireland, and during the eighteenth century it enjoyed a greater degree of security than at any period since the reformation. This did not lead to any considerable expansion. The civil power was satisfied to safeguard the church without attempting to enforce uniformity and the church itself showed little missionary zeal. Some Roman catholics of the land-owning class conformed under pressure of the penal laws and a few presbyterians with political ambitions did the same, but the bulk of the people were unaffected. In the early part of the century the church was active in struggling for the rights of convocation and for internal reform. But the government's policy of appointing English whig bishops to the more important sees soon produced a change, and though the spirit of tory high churchmanship never quite disappeared, the church establishment came to be regarded as little more than a department of state. Indirectly, however, the church could still exercise a strong influence through parliament, as appears, for example, in its resistance to the removal of the sacramental test.

The Irish parliament was able to maintain the strictly Anglican character of the protestant ascendancy, even against the pressure of English whig governments, because it had itself acquired a new importance. In the later middle ages it had represented little more than the four 'obedient shires'. During the sixteenth century it represented a progressively wider area, but its meetings became infrequent and irregular; in Elizabeth's reign, for example, there were only three, and each was called to deal with some specific question. Wentworth's attempt to use parliament as a normal instrument of government was intended solely for the benefit of the crown, and the experiment was a short one. At the restoration, the Irish parliament had a chance of acquiring the same sort of influence as the English, for the hereditary revenue was now hopelessly insufficient to meet the cost of government. But parliament increased this revenue so generously that the king was made independent of further supply, and the opportunity was lost. By 1692, however, government expenditure had once more got ahead of income, and this time, instead of increasing the hereditary revenue again, parliament granted 'additional duties' for a limited period. In Anne's reign it became the established practice to grant these duties for two years at a time, and thenceforward parliament had to be called at least every second year. It was therefore not until after the revolution that Ireland became in fact what she had long been in theory, a parliamentary monarchy. The Irish parliament had thus little more than a century of continuous existence. The rapidity with which it built

up its traditions and the degree of maturity which it attained in
that brief period are far more remarkable than the corruption
and bigotry which are often the only things remembered about it.
During the seventeenth century it had managed, in spite of
Poynings' law, to establish some degree of initiative in legislation,
by the practice of introducing 'heads of bills', and by the early
eighteenth century this had become the normal procedure. These
'heads' were bills in all but form, and could be freely debated and
amended. If passed, they were submitted to the lord lieutenant
and council to be approved first by them, then by the king and
council in England and so sent back to be laid before parliament.
It was a clumsy and defective procedure. Heads of a bill might be
suppressed or altered in either council. If they were suppressed
parliament had no remedy; if altered, it could only accept or
reject the bill in its new form.

This parliament was not, in any modern democratic sense,
representative of the country, or even of the Anglican minority.
There were boroughs as 'rotten' as any in England: Clonmines
had only one house, Harristown had none at all, Bannow was a
mountain of sea-sand. Even in boroughs which had a larger
population the parliamentary franchise was often confined to
a small group, under the control of a 'patron' who was usually
a neighbouring landlord. The buying and selling of seats was at
least as widely practised as in England. The county elections were
often genuine contests, but they were contests between landlords;
for though the forty-shilling freeholders held the franchise, the
great majority of them were so completely under the control of
their landlords that they could be counted on to vote as they were
directed. Another factor which limited the representative character
of the Irish parliament was the infrequency of general elections.
There was no triennial or septennial act, and parliament might
last until dissolved by the demise of the crown. One parliament
lasted throughout the reign of George I, another throughout the
reign of George II.

In many respects the Irish parliament bore a strong resem-
blance to the English, but there was a fundamental difference
between the constitutions of the two kingdoms. In Ireland, the
executive, centred in the lord lieutenant, was imposed from outside. Parliament might accept or reject the lord lieutenant's
policy but could not get rid of him, for he was the nominee of
the English ministry of the day. During the first half of the

eighteenth century he was normally an absentee, coming over at two-yearly intervals to conduct a session of parliament. The visit generally lasted about six months and was almost wholly taken up in the management of the house of commons; for his great task was to form and maintain a government party which would defend him from attack and ensure that the necessary legislation, above all the supply bills, got through safely. It was impossible to calculate in advance how things would go, for since the exclusion of the recusants in the seventeenth century clear party divisions had disappeared. There was a body of place-holders, on whom the government could usually rely, and there was a solid core of malcontents—'the standing, sour opposition of the house', as a contemporary called them; there was an ill-defined group of 'country gentlemen'—composed mainly, though not exclusively, of county members—who usually supported the government from a sense of duty as well as from hope of reward; but the general character of the house appears most clearly in the comparison of it to a highland army, a collection of clans or groups, each gathered round a chief. The rival ambitions and shifting alliances of these groups formed the pattern of parliamentary politics.

To build up a government majority out of such discordant elements was an exhausting task and involved protracted negotiations with everyone who had or might have influence in the house. The most constant element in the situation was the selfishness of the members, whose support had generally to be secured by titles, places and pensions for themselves, and civil, military and ecclesiastical appointments for their relations. A majority so composed was apt to disintegrate, and throughout the session the lord lieutenant had an almost daily struggle to hold it together under the stress of internal rivalries and personal ambitions.

There was another, and greater, danger, against which it was difficult to guard in advance. Both in parliament and in the country there was a continuous, though fluctuating, tradition of patriotism, an 'Irish interest', as opposed to the 'English interest' of the government. Any measure which caught the popular imagination as detrimental to Ireland might lead to public demonstrations in Dublin, and a flood of protests from grand juries and corporations throughout the country. The house of commons, in spite of its unrepresentative character and the

selfishness of its members, could sometimes be very sensitive to
this sort of public opinion; a vigorous opposition might spring
up and sweep into its ranks the bulk of the government's allies,
until even the very place-men, whose duty it was to support the
lord lieutenant through thick and thin, would hesitate to stand
out against the popular will. But an opposition of this sort had
even less cohesion than the mercenary majority of the government. The lord lieutenant had only to wait for the excitement to
subside, reconstruct his party and go on as before: the Irish house
of commons might, on occasion, defeat the policy of the ministry,
but could not drive it from office.

2. THE ECONOMIC PROBLEM

During the eighteenth century Ireland enjoyed a longer period of
internal peace than ever before. There were local agrarian disturbances, which sometimes reached serious proportions, but
from the treaty of Limerick to the insurrection of 1798 there was
no general threat to the existing order. Yet this prolonged peace
did not make the country really prosperous. One traveller after
another comments on the lack of capital, the scarcity of profitable employment, the swarms of beggars in the towns, the meagre
fare and wretched hovels of the bulk of the rural population.
There was some improvement in the last quarter of the century,
but even then Ireland compared very unfavourably with England.

This state of affairs requires some explanation. Ireland was a
fertile country and during the brief period of peace which followed
the restoration had made considerable economic progress. There
was a natural set-back at the revolution, when agriculture,
manufactures and trade were all disrupted; but it might have been
expected that the re-establishment of peace would have led to a
sustained recovery. The fact that this did not happen has most
commonly been attributed to the English policy of restricting
Irish manufactures, and especially the woollen manufacture,
which at this time was very prosperous. In 1699 an act of the
English parliament prohibited the export of woollen goods from
Ireland to any country except England, from which they were
already virtually excluded by very heavy duties. Under this blow
the Irish industry quickly withered away. The motive behind the
act was partly commercial jealousy, for English manufacturers
were alarmed at the competition of Irish goods in the continental

market, and partly the fear that an over-prosperous Ireland might yield the crown an independent revenue. The protestant ascendancy was naturally indignant at this new assertion of the English parliament's claim to pass acts binding on Ireland, and the restriction of the woollen trade became one of its standing grievances on constitutional as well as on economic grounds. Partly on this account the practical effects of the restriction were greatly exaggerated. At the most prosperous period of the industry woollen goods formed only a small proportion of total exports, and Irish manufacturers supplied only a fraction even of the home market. On the other hand, the industry was a growing one and had attracted both workmen and capital from England. Its restriction was a discouragement to further enterprise, and though it is not likely that Ireland would ever have become an important manufacturing country, the presence of a prosperous woollen industry, even on a small scale, would have improved the whole economic situation.

As a compensation for restricting the woollen industry the English parliament expressed its readiness to encourage the manufacture of linen, which did not compete with any English interest, and something was done in this direction with the help of protestant refugees from France, of whom many thousands settled in Ireland. At first progress was slow, but the Irish parliament made great efforts to promote the industry, and England conceded some preferences to Irish linen both in the home market and in the colonies. By the end of the first quarter of the century linen was second in importance only to provisions in the list of Irish exports, and accounted for almost one third of their total value. But the industry, though established in other areas also, was mainly concentrated in the north, so that its benefits were localised. A freely-developing woollen industry might have spread the same sort of benefits over the rest of the country.

The restrictions on trade, though not directly responsible for the poverty of Ireland, contributed to it by emphasising the country's economic dependence on agriculture at a time when the population was steadily increasing. The vital statistics of the period are a matter of conjecture rather than of accurate calculation; but it seems reasonably certain that the population increased from under 2,000,000 at the beginning of the eighteenth century to about 2,500,000 in the middle and over 4,000,000 at the close.[1] It is true that Ireland could have supported the increased population comfortably enough, even on a purely rural economy, if the land had been efficiently farmed. But agricultural methods in general use were far behind those of England, and social and economic conditions alike were against any improvement. Behind this inefficiency lay the essential causes of Ireland's poverty. A great many of the landlords, especially the more important, were absentees, either because their principal estates lay in England, or because, as comparative new-comers, they had little interest in Ireland and preferred the life of London or Bath to that of Dublin or the Irish country-side. Whether absentees or not, most Irish landlords were satisfied to draw what they could from their lands and give little or nothing in return. There were, of course, a few 'improving' landlords among them, and in 1731 some of the more enthusiastic formed the Dublin Society,[2] which experimented with new methods, provided better implements, offered bounties for planting of trees, and generally encouraged a more profitable use of land. The society did much valuable work; but the vast majority of Irish tenant farmers were too poor, and held by too uncertain a tenure, to benefit from its encouragement and advice.

The poverty and insecurity of the tenant farmers were the great economic evils of the situation. They were closely connected and had a common origin in the mounting pressure upon land, almost the only source of livelihood. Even the landlord class did not wholly escape this pressure; for though the greater landlords could secure a steady income with little trouble by letting out their estates in large tracts, on long leases and at moderate rents, the 'middlemen' who took up these leases were often people who in England might have invested their money in commerce, but in Ireland had to make a living out of land. They sub-let, necessarily on shorter leases and at higher rents. There were sometimes several such sub-lettings between the original landlord and the actual cultivator of the soil, who seldom had a longer lease than thirty-one years, and was sometimes a yearly tenant with no lease at all. His rent was exorbitant, for several profits had to come out of it; as a result, he rarely had any capital, and he could

1. These are the traditional estimates. Recent research suggests that they are too low, and puts the population at over 2,500,000 at the beginning of the century, over 3,000,000 in the middle, and over 4,750,000 at the end. (K. H. Connell, *The population of Ireland, 1750–1845*, Oxford, 1950, p. 25.)
2. Now the Royal Dublin Society.

expect no help from his landlord; but if by his own labour he improved the value of his holding the rent would almost certainly be increased when the lease fell in, or he might be evicted without compensation in favour of someone else. Wretched as these conditions were, the demand for farms was so great that tenants would offer almost any rent for the sake of a bare subsistence.

This state of affairs was made worse by a steady decline in the area under cultivation. The export of provisions and the smuggling of wool to France were two of the most flourishing trades in the country, and both encouraged pasture at the expense of tillage to a degree that alarmed many public-spirited observers. Bishop Berkeley, for example, asks in his *Querist*,[1] 'Whether a great quantity of sheep-walk be not ruinous to a country?' The same fear was expressed by Swift, and by many less illustrious writers, but it was not until towards the close of the century that the decline in tillage was checked, partly by legislation and partly by the increased English demand for imported grain. But any advantage which this might have brought to the Irish peasantry was off-set by the steady growth of population, so that the pressure upon land was as heavy as before. Even the decline of the middleman system about this time brought no relief. Landlords took to managing their estates through agents, but rents rose higher than ever, and conditions of tenure showed no signs of improvement.

The encroachment of pasture upon arable meant that farms had to be subdivided to meet the needs of the growing population; and the process continued, despite the later increase in the area under tillage, until a large proportion of the tenantry had sunk to the position of mere cottiers, scraping a miserable livelihood from a couple of acres of rack-rented land. The cottier system has been described as 'serfdom reduced to a money standard and modified by competition'. Labour was set against rent, but the value of both was calculated in money. Since land was scarce and labour plentiful the balance was heavily weighted against the tenant and he had sometimes to make up a portion of the rent in cash. Small as their holdings were, few cottiers could consume the best of their own products. The butter and eggs, the pig and the poultry were sold, and the family lived on potatoes and buttermilk. In normal years there was at least a sufficient quantity of this simple

1. A series of questions relating to the condition of Ireland, first published in 1735.

food, and Arthur Young, who visited Ireland in the 1770s, thought the Irish cottier in this respect better off than the English agricultural labourer. The sufficiency of the food supply, together with the apparent hopelessness of expecting any improvement in the standard of living, encouraged early marriages and large families. Only the potato could have met the needs of this expanding population, for no other food crop gives such a heavy yield in proportion to the area it occupies.[1] But there was no margin of safety and a single bad harvest was enough to threaten a great part of the population with starvation. In 1727–9 there was a period of acute scarcity throughout the south and west; and in 1740 and 1741 there was an actual famine, in which mortality was undoubtedly very high, though it can hardly have reached the figure of 400,000, suggested by some contemporaries. Even in normal times the rate of mortality was high and fevers were endemic, for the living conditions of the peasantry were wretched, even by the standards of eighteenth-century England or France. The poorest of them lived in mud cabins, scarcely fit to keep out the rain, with a cesspool before the door, and containing a single room which the half-naked family shared with the cow, the pig and the hens. Even those who were better-off lived in conditions scarcely more sanitary. It was no wonder that epidemics arose easily and spread widely.

In the north the position of the tenant farmer was rather better than in the rest of the country. There he had some security of tenure and some encouragement to make improvements, for the 'Ulster custom' protected him against eviction and undue increase of rent, and entitled him to sell his interest in his farm when he left it. The custom had no legal force, but was so strongly supported by public opinion that few landlords dared to ignore it, and in general it was as profitable to them as to the tenants; rents in Ulster were more regularly paid than elsewhere, and the value of the tenant's saleable interest was a security against arrears. The presence of the linen industry was another advantage to the north. It increased the amount of money in general circulation, and many small farmers and cottiers found in weaving an additional employment which released them from complete dependence upon the land. But though the north was better off than the rest of Ireland, it was neither contented nor prosperous,

1. Arthur Young calculated that it would have taken four times the acreage to maintain the same population on wheat. (*Tour in Ireland*, ed. 1892, ii. 46.)

and there was a steady emigration to the American colonies during the half-century before the war of independence. These Ulster emigrants, almost all of them presbyterians, left home with a sense of grievance against the government, and their influence helped to push the colonists along the path to complete independence.

Agrarian crime was the natural result of the wretchedness and insecurity of the peasants, but it did not become generally serious until the latter half of the century. The turning-point was 1759 when the restrictions on the importation of Irish cattle into England were removed. The expansion of pasture, which had been going on steadily for so long, was now suddenly speeded up, and a few years later the removal of similar restrictions on Irish provisions helped to maintain the process. Tenants were turned off their farms, whole villages were swept away and common lands were enclosed. It was in these circumstances that the 'Whiteboy' movement arose—an organised campaign of terror, directed in the first place against enclosures, but soon concerning itself with all the grievances of the peasantry. The movement began in Tipperary and spread over much of Munster and Leinster. It varied in ferocity from time to time, but despite stern action by the government and the magistrates it was never really rooted out, and the tradition of mutilation and murder as the tenant's redress for grievance survived into the nineteenth century. The better conditions in the north protected it from such serious and prolonged unrest. The 'Oakboys' in mid-Ulster and the 'Steelboys' (or 'Hearts of steel') in county Antrim were produced by local and temporary grievances, and the organisations disappeared when the immediate causes passed away.

Contemporary opinion was inclined to attribute the Whiteboy movement to foreign political intrigue; but there is little evidence to support this suspicion, and even less likelihood that the Irish peasantry of the southern provinces would have responded to any political appeal. Along the west coast a connection with France was still maintained and men were still being recruited for the French service; there was even a lingering Jacobite tradition in the songs of the Gaelic poets. But the whole body of the peasantry was politically inert. Even the survival of the Irish language had, at this stage, little political significance, for the literary tradition was aristocratic, and the Irish-speaking aristo-

cracy had almost wholly disappeared. With them had gone the
vital force of the Gaelic-nationalist tradition, and it contributed
almost nothing to the disastrous efforts at the close of the
eighteenth century and the opening of the nineteenth to establish
an independent Ireland.

The poverty of Ireland, obvious enough to the traveller
through the countryside, was not absolutely unrelieved. Despite
restrictions and difficulties trade expanded fairly steadily during
the first half of the century, and from the 1760s onwards the
expansion was rapid. Towns increased in size and importance,
new roads were constructed and land rose in value. But this
wealth was almost entirely in the hands of landlords and merchants; and so many of the landlords were absentees who spent
their incomes abroad that the annual drain of rents from the
country more than swallowed up an otherwise favourable balance
of trade. The perpetual shortage of capital which resulted was
one of the main reasons for the under-development of Ireland's
resources. There were some signs of improvement in the last
twenty years of the century, when more landlords were living at
home and a middle class, mainly lawyers and merchants, was
rising in wealth and influence. But the radical weaknesses
remained. The population, now growing more rapidly than ever,
was still almost wholly dependent upon agriculture; and the superficial prosperity of a small class went only a short way towards
providing the capital and the security which the country needed.
    The almost universal scarcity of money was of some advantage
to the resident gentry; labour and provisions were so cheap that
they could employ troops of servants and entertain on a lavish
scale. English visitors were chiefly impressed by the prodigal
display and the disorder that often accompanied it, and the lesser
gentry in particular were certainly given to drunkenness and
duelling. But the splendid Georgian mansions still standing in
many parts of the country are evidence of the good taste as well
as of the extravagance of the eighteenth-century landlords. The
same good taste appears in some of the country towns, but its
fullest expression is naturally in Dublin, which depends for its
architectural interest almost entirely upon the public buildings,
the great mansions, and the residential squares of the eighteenth
century. Dublin was at this time the second city in the British
Isles and was the equal of any of the smaller European capitals,

not only in its architecture but in the variety and refinement of
its social life.

This Anglo-Irish civilisation suffered from the attractive power
of England and (as Froude says) Ireland lost as much by the
absenteeism of her men of genius as of her landlords, a loss of
which Burke, Goldsmith and Sheridan are perhaps the outstanding examples of this century. Swift and Bishop Berkeley
remained at home; and though with the former at least this was a
matter of necessity and not of choice, they both devoted some
part of their genius to the service of their native land. But throughout the whole eighteenth century Ireland had an intellectual life
of her own which found expression in literature and scholarship.
Dublin, with Trinity College, was naturally the most important
centre, but in some of the provincial towns also, notably Belfast,
there was a good deal of intellectual activity in the last quarter of
the century. And in one respect at least Ireland could face any
comparison: the oratory of her house of commons, though
different in character, was certainly not inferior in quality to that
of the British, even in the age of Pitt and Fox.

Few Irishmen of the period, even among the educated classes,
realised fully how precarious was the foundation upon which the
whole structure of their society stood. But some of the evils of the
economic position were obvious to all, and it was natural to
attribute them to the restrictions imposed by authority of the
English parliament. From the reign of William III onwards the
demand for legislative independence was linked with the com-
plaint that Ireland's natural development was being thwarted by
English control.

3. THE WINNING OF A CONSTITUTION

The discontent of the protestant ascendancy naturally found
expression in parliament, which in spite of all its defects as a
representative assembly could always provide a platform for the
assertion of Irish rights. From the revolution onwards it had
struggled intermittently to establish two claims: the first was its
own sole right to legislate for Ireland; the second, the principle
that supply bills should not be drawn up in England and presented
ready-made, but should take their rise in the form of 'heads' in
the Irish house of commons. The former claim was laid down by

William Molyneux in his *Case of Ireland's being bound by acts of parliament in England, stated*,[1] a book which the English commons immediately condemned for its 'bold and pernicious assertions' of Ireland's legislative independence. But the claim still remained, and in George I's reign the English parliament tried to quash it finally by a declaratory act asserting its own authority 'to make laws and statutes of sufficient force and validity to bind the kingdom and people of Ireland'.[2] The question of the supply bills also became a matter of serious dispute during the 1690s and the struggle continued, in various forms, for the next sixty or seventy years.

Though the lord lieutenant could generally, by means already indicated, secure a majority in the house of commons, the task was always more difficult when these or other matters affecting the constitution or welfare of Ireland were at issue, for on such occasions the Irish interest would receive many recruits in the house and much noisy support in the country. The inconvenience which this might cause the government was demonstrated in the prolonged struggle over 'Wood's halfpence' which lasted from 1723 to 1725. Ireland was short of copper coinage, and authority to coin halfpence and farthings was granted to William Wood of Wolverhampton. There was an immediate outcry in Ireland against the manner in which the grant was made, against the quality of the coins and against the quantity to be issued. Public feeling, once aroused, could not be kept within the limits of the original dispute. Swift, in his *Drapier's letters*, raised the whole question of Anglo-Irish relationships, and indignantly denied that 'the people of Ireland are in some sort of slavery or dependence different from those of England'. This dangerous excitement was shared by the Irish parliament. In the house of commons the government could not find a single member to oppose the demand for an inquiry into the grant, and even the most docile office-holders would do no more than attempt to tone down the addresses against it which both lords and commons presented to the king. In the end the government had to give way; the lord lieutenant was recalled and another sent over in his place to announce that Wood's authority had been revoked. The constitutional agitation, deprived of its immediate stimulus, now died

1. Published in Dublin, 1698.
2. This statute, generally known as the 'sixth of George I', also took away the appellate jurisdiction of the Irish house of lords.

as quickly as it had arisen. But the government did not ignore the lesson of its defeat; and during the next decade a more efficient way of managing the house of commons was gradually worked out. The lord lieutenant ceased to take direct responsibility for building up and maintaining a government party, and left the task to two or three of the leading members of parliament. These 'undertakers' guaranteed to put through government business, especially the granting of supplies, and in return they were entrusted with a considerable share of crown patronage. The undertaker system restricted the authority and lowered the prestige of the lord lieutenant, but it assured him a quiet session during his six months' visit to Ireland. From the Irish point of view, the system had at least the advantage of preserving some patronage for Irishmen, at a period when it was the usual practice to appoint Englishmen to almost all posts of importance in Ireland. But, on the other hand, the regular management of the house of commons by undertakers made it difficult for any strong and consistent patriotic opposition to establish itself. The Irish interest lived on, but it was not until the undertaker system was on the decline that it won any notable success.

The undertakers were entrusted with the management of parliament for the specific purpose of securing the passage of government measures, but they soon developed a distinct interest of their own, based on their parliamentary influence. 'The lord lieutenant', says Charlemont, 'was wholly in their power, and could confer no favour but at their recommendation.'[1] Any attempt on his part to rely upon other advisers would produce the threat of a dangerous revolt. In some respects the situation resembled that in the early Tudor period, when government was left in the hands of an Anglo-Irish noble who maintained royal authority in return for a considerable degree of independence. In the sixteenth century the only alternative to the rule of Kildare was the appointment of a strong English chief governor, backed up by an English army; in the eighteenth century the only alternative to the undertakers was a resident lord lieutenant backed up by the full authority of the British government. But this alternative would have required a strong and consistent Irish policy such as no British government of the period was capable of producing.

1. James Caulfeild, first earl of Charlemont, was the political ally of Flood and Grattan, and commander-in-chief of the volunteers. See below.

Something of the character of Irish political life at this time can be seen in the course of a parliamentary dispute of the 1750s. The Irish parliament claimed the right to dispose of surplus revenue. The British government denied this and insisted that it was a royal prerogative. The excitement, both in parliament and in the country, was as great as that aroused over Wood's patent, and in some respects it was more dangerous, for the undertakers themselves turned against the lord lieutenant, espoused the popular cause and brought about the defeat of the government in the house of commons. But though this dispute showed how easily patriotic, or at least anti-English, feelings could be aroused among the Irish gentry and the Dublin mob, its conclusion showed also how completely the country was lacking in constructive leadership. The undertakers had appealed to these feelings almost entirely for selfish ends. They felt their monopoly of influence threatened by the political machinations of the primate, George Stone, and were anxious to convince the lord lieutenant that they were indispensable to the peaceful conduct of affairs. In this they were at least partially successful. The most important of them, Henry Boyle, speaker of the house of commons, was bought off with an earldom and a pension, and his chief colleagues were similarly satisfied. The deserted patriots had no alternative leaders to turn to, and were obliged to vent their feelings in execrations; the mob, which had once escorted Boyle in triumph from the parliament to his house, now, with equal enthusiasm, burnt him in effigy.

The disappointment of the mob was justified, but the constitutional questions which had been raised were not entirely lost sight of. In the words of Lord Charlemont, Irishmen 'were taught that Ireland had, or ought to have, a constitution'. Within ten years the lesson had been learnt and under more efficient and honester leaders the Irish interest began to acquire some of the cohesion of a patriot party. Charles Lucas, the 'Wilkes of Ireland', after a long career of agitation against abuses in public life, entered parliament for the city of Dublin in 1761. Henry Flood, a much younger and abler man, entered in 1759. The immediate objects for which they and their allies struggled were security of tenure for the judges, the passage of a habeas corpus act, the establishment of a national militia and the limitation of the life of parliament.

This desire to share in constitutional privileges long enjoyed in England was typical of the patriots' outlook. Though determined to establish the rights of Ireland they had no thought of separation. They were proud of their English origin and regarded England and Ireland as sister-kingdoms, held together by loyalty to the same crown and entitled to the same liberties. As the confederation of Kilkenny in 1642 had appealed to Magna Carta, so they appealed to the traditional rights of English citizens. 'Am I a free man in England', asked Swift, 'and do I become a slave in six hours by crossing the channel?' This insistence upon the English connection was typical of protestant nationalism. Its protestantism was no less important. Many of its leaders were bitterly opposed to the claims of the Roman catholics, and even those who favoured their admission to political privileges were determined, at the same time, to maintain a protestant ascendancy. 'I love the Roman catholic', said Grattan, in response to a protestant address from the corporation of Dublin, 'I am a friend to his liberty, but it is only inasmuch as his liberty is entirely consistent with your ascendancy, and an addition to the strength and freedom of the protestant community.'

The ultimate success of the patriots resulted, in part at least, from a change in British policy towards Ireland. Early in the reign of George III the British government decided to break the independent power of the undertakers by appointing a resident lord lieutenant who would have effective control of the administration. It was not easy to find the right man; but in 1767 Lord Townshend was sent over and remained continuously in Ireland until 1772. By that time, he had carried through his task, and thenceforward the lord lieutenant himself was the great dispenser of patronage and the active manager of the house of commons. The patriots gained one immediate advantage from Townshend's policy. Partly to gain popularity, partly to undermine the influence of the undertakers, he had supported the demand for a limitation of the life of parliament, an octennial act had been passed in 1768, and the patriots naturally benefited from the resulting increase of popular influence in the house of commons. But the final suppression of the undertakers produced a far more significant result. The lord lieutenant was now brought directly into the political conflict, and as the representative not only of the king but also of the British government he was the symbol of that dependence of Ireland upon England which the patriots so strongly resented. The government found it increasingly difficult to play off one Irish party against another and was eventually forced into a decisive trial of strength, in which all the discontented elements in the country were ranged on the patriot side.

Townshend's victory over the undertakers came at a time when the difficulties of Irish government were increasing. Heavy expenditure during the Seven Years' War had raised the national debt to an unprecedented figure, and this not only provided a target for popular criticism, but made it more important than ever to secure regular and substantial parliamentary supplies. The dispute with the American colonists made things worse. Irishmen were naturally interested in a country with whose population they had such close family ties, and they could not help recognising that the constitutional question was directly relevant to their own situation. As a Dublin newspaper expressed it: 'By the same authority which the British parliament assumes to tax America, it may also and with equal justice presume to tax Ireland without the consent or concurrence of the Irish parliament.' It was, however, some time before the patriots were able to turn the situation to advantage. Even in 1775, after war had actually begun, Flood accepted the post of vice-treasurer, convinced that the policy of opposition was a barren one and that he could gain more for the country in office. But the patriots continued their policy under the leadership of Henry Grattan, who entered parliament in the same year and whose eloquence at once raised him to a position of great influence.

Circumstances were now working in the opposition's favour. The dislocation of trade and the rise in prices produced by the war resulted in bankruptcies, distress and unemployment. The patriots at once attributed these evils to a government embargo on the export of provisions, though in fact the provision trade (which supplied the armed forces) was more flourishing than ever. The truth or falsehood of the patriot propaganda mattered little, the important thing was that it aroused bitter resentment against England, concentrated public attention on commercial restrictions and led to an almost universal demand for 'free trade'. In this way Ireland's constitutional claims were closely associated with material grievances and a vigorous public opinion was maintained. A strong government might still have controlled the situation. But Buckinghamshire, the lord lieutenant, though by no means the 'fluttered imbecile' which Froude called him, was not a strong man in a crisis, and Lord North, almost over-

whelmed with domestic and foreign difficulties, gave him very
uncertain backing. The entry of France into the war and the
consequent threat of invasion revealed the full helplessness of
government in Ireland. Most of the troops had been withdrawn;
though a militia act had been passed, there was no money to put
it into force; privateers were swarming around the coasts and even
communications with England were unsafe. It was clear that if
the French did come the people of Ireland would have to depend
upon themselves, and out of this state of affairs sprang the
volunteer movement.

The first regular company was formed in Belfast early in 1778;
by the end of the year this example had been followed over the
whole kingdom, and so, instead of a militia under government
control, there came into existence a national volunteer army.
The volunteers were exclusively protestant. For the most part they
were merchants, tradesmen and well-to-do farmers, officered by
the nobility and gentry; to use Grattan's phrase, they represented
'the armed property of the nation'. The government could neither
disband nor control them. They were responsible to no authority
save that of their own councils and conventions, but they professed
great respect for the Irish parliament, and the patriot opposition soon
found in them both a fresh weapon and a fresh stimulus to action.

The French invasion did not come, and it may have been
partly because they were not called on for active service that the
volunteers turned so readily to politics. From the first they had
taken a particular interest in the trade question. Their uniforms
were all of Irish cloth. Their councils passed resolutions and
drank toasts in favour of 'a free trade for Ireland'. In the autumn
of 1779, when parliament met, they gave more forcible expression
to these sentiments. While the house of commons demanded
free trade and voted supplies for six months only, the volunteers
held a great parade in Dublin (significantly, it was to com-
memorate the birthday of the protestant hero, William III) and
decorated their brass cannon with the threatening placard 'Free
trade—or else'. Such an onslaught, combined with the almost
desperate condition of British arms in America and of tory
politics at home, forced Lord North to make concessions, and
acts were passed through the British parliament removing most
of the restrictions on Irish trade.

The victory was great, but insecure and even dangerous. It
was based partly on the temporary weakness of the British

government and partly on the support of the volunteers. But
the government might recover, and the same authority which
had removed the restrictions might reimpose them. The volunteers had been easy to arouse, but would it be possible to control
them? For the time being it was the former question which
engaged the attention of the patriots. Lord North had spoken of
the trade concessions as 'resumable', and it was urged in Ireland
that the only way to guarantee their permanence was to establish
the exclusive right of the Irish parliament to legislate for Ireland.
But a resolution to this effect, moved in the commons by Grattan
early in 1780, was heavily defeated, for the excitement of 1779
had died down and the lord lieutenant and his agents had succeeded in rebuilding a government majority. In the following
year attempts to secure the modification of Poynings' law failed
also, though Flood, now once more in opposition, supported
them. From these parliamentary defeats the patriot leaders turned
to the volunteers. In February 1782 a convention of delegates
from the volunteer corps of Ulster met at Dungannon and passed
a series of political resolutions drawn up by Grattan, Flood and
Charlemont. The most important were those which asserted the sole
right of the Irish parliament to legislate for Ireland and declared that
the powers exercised by the privy councils of the two kingdoms
under Poynings' law were 'unconstitutional and a grievance'.

The armed force behind this declaration made it formidable,
but its speedy fulfilment was due quite as much to a change of
government in Great Britain. In March 1782 Lord North resigned
and was succeeded by a whig ministry under Rockingham.
Though the whigs were sympathetic towards the Irish claims and
though some of the new ministers were in friendly touch with the
patriot leaders, it is doubtful how much of the Dungannon
programme they would have conceded if they had been given
time for negotiation. But Ireland was in a state of expectancy
which would not tolerate delay. Before the whigs had been a
month in office, and when the new lord lieutenant whom they
sent over had been barely two days in Dublin, the Irish parliament
met, and an address to the king, which was virtually a declaration of independence, was moved in the house of commons by
Grattan and carried unanimously.

Whatever hesitation the government may have felt before, it
now yielded completely, and within a brief space the British
and Irish parliaments passed a series of acts which placed the

constitutional relations between the two kingdoms on a new footing. The British parliament, by repealing the 'sixth of George I', virtually gave up its claim to legislate for Ireland. An act of the Irish parliament (usually known as 'Yelverton's act') drastically modified Poynings' law. In future, the lord lieutenant and council in Ireland were to transmit to England, without alteration, all measures submitted to them by the Irish parliament, and no others. But the powers of the king and council in England were not entirely taken away; though they were not to alter or add to a bill they might suppress it altogether.[1] Other measures provided for the independence of the Irish courts and for the security of tenure of the judges. All these measures taken together form what is often called 'the constitution of 1782'. But it was neither, like the British constitution, a matter of growth, nor, like the American, a coherent system set out in a single instrument. The rights which it secured to the Irish parliament were greater in theory than in practice and its weaknesses were fully revealed during the eighteen years of its existence.

4. GRATTAN'S PARLIAMENT AND THE LEGISLATIVE UNION

The years between 1782 and 1800 are generally referred to as the period of 'Grattan's parliament', and, though many other people contributed to the establishment of parliamentary independence, there is justice in the title. Grattan represented much of what was best in the Anglo-Irish tradition, though he was not entirely free from its characteristic faults. It was he who had led the patriot opposition during the difficult years that preceded the formation of the volunteers; it was he who had brought the force of volunteer opinion to bear upon the government; it was he who had carried through the parliamentary campaign which had led to success; and it was he who had launched parliament on its new career of liberty in one of his most famous speeches: 'I found Ireland on her knees, I watched over her with a paternal solicitude; I have traced her progress from injuries to arms, and from arms to liberty. . . . Ireland is now a nation. In that new character I hail her, and bowing to her august presence I say, *Esto perpetua!*'

With the opening of the new era there came a quickening of economic recovery. The removal of trade restrictions in 1779

1. In practice, this power of suppressing bills was allowed to lapse.

had not brought much immediate benefit, but the effect was increasingly felt during the next few years. Existing industries expanded; and the woollen manufacture, which had been almost destroyed at the end of the seventeenth century, now revived rapidly, though it failed to establish a large export trade. Not unnaturally, parliamentary independence came to be associated in the public mind with national prosperity; and it is certainly true that parliament did try to encourage trade and industry, and especially agriculture, upon which the prosperity of Ireland must always in the long run depend. An act of 1784 ('Foster's corn law') marked a turning-point in the long struggle between pasture and tillage. By a system of bounties it encouraged the growth of corn, and more and more land was brought under cultivation. In another way, also, the country drew economic advantage from the establishment of parliamentary independence, for the increased prestige of the Irish parliament led many former absentees to spend more of their time and money in Ireland, and especially in Dublin, which now reached the height of its fame and splendour as a capital. The country towns also felt something of the same influence, and one traveller after another remarks on the widespread signs of increasing prosperity.

All this prosperity, real though it was, did nothing to better the lot of the peasant. He still suffered from rack-renting and from insecurity of tenure; he had little chance and no encouragement to accumulate capital for the improvement of his holding. The increase of tillage was of benefit chiefly to the landlords. Many of them had by now given up the middleman system and taken the management of their estates into their own hands, either directly or through agents. But this proved of little advantage to the cultivators of the soil, who lived as before at the level of bare subsistence. At least, however, the increase of tillage meant that more farms were available, not only because more land was cultivated but also because the greater profit meant that a rent and a living could be squeezed out of a smaller area. As a result, the practice of subdividing holdings became more and more common, especially after the French war had pushed up the price of farm produce. At the same time there was a steep rise in population.[1] This may have owed something to the process

1. According to K. H. Connell (*The population of Ireland, 1750–1845*, Oxford, 1950) the rise in population, though rapid, was not so sudden as has generally been supposed. Cf. above, p. 106.

of subdivision, which made early marriages more easily possible, but in turn it forced on the process to an extent which was to produce disaster in the nineteenth century.

The poverty and discontent of the countryside expressed itself, as usual, in agrarian crime. The Whiteboy movement reappeared in Munster. In the north, the pressure of competition for farms, which was still considerable, led to sectarian quarrels between Roman catholics and protestants. But in spite of such reminders politicians paid little attention to the social problems of the peasantry. English interest and Irish interest, reformers and anti-reformers alike confined themselves almost entirely to constitutional questions. It was the claims of the kingdom of Ireland, rather than the welfare of the bulk of the inhabitants, that engrossed their attention. But the agrarian problem could not safely be ignored, and the fatal weakness of the ascendancy system during the critical years at the end of the century resulted almost as much from social and economic as from political factors.

Despite the enthusiasm which greeted the 'constitution of 1782' the position was neither satisfactory nor stable. There was no firm basis of agreement among Irish politicians. Many had been swept reluctantly along by the rising tide of nationalist fervour, and had supported the cause of parliamentary independence merely because they saw the hopelessness of opposition and wished to be on the winning side. Even among the victorious patriots there were deep differences of opinion. This was natural enough, but the personal ambition of Flood made the situation dangerous. Since his return to opposition in 1779 he had struggled hard to recover his former leadership, and to this end had constantly pressed his demands beyond the limits proposed by Grattan. He refused to be satisfied with the concessions made by the British government in 1782 and asserted that the new-found liberty of the Irish parliament was not secure, that the repeal of the 'sixth of George I' was not enough, that if the British parliament had had the right to legislate for Ireland before that act was passed the right was not affected by simple repeal. He therefore demanded that the British parliament should also renounce explicitly any claim to bind Ireland. Flood's argument may have had some legal justification, but it was impolitic to press victory to its utmost limits; and though he had his way, the renunciation act which the British parliament passed in 1783 added nothing to the real security of Irish freedom.

There was more serious and more lasting difference among the patriots on the question of parliamentary reform. Here again Flood went beyond Grattan both in end and method. Grattan had expressed the hope that the volunteers, their work accomplished, would leave parliament to use the freedom they had won for it; Flood, on the other hand, was foremost among those who urged them to continue their political activities until parliament itself had been reformed. In 1783 he asked permission of the house of commons to bring in a reform bill which had the support of a volunteer convention then assembled in Dublin. But the house was not disposed to share its authority and refused permission, on the ground that to grant it would be to submit to external pressure. There was sound reason in this, but natural selfishness had at least as much to do with the decision; placemen and borough-owners had no desire for parliamentary reform. This rebuff, and their own internal disagreements, rapidly weakened the political influence of the volunteers, and the demand for parliamentary reform fell temporarily into the background.

The discussion of parliamentary reform inevitably brought forward the question of admitting Roman catholics to political power, and the bitter differences which were immediately revealed indicate one of the fundamental weaknesses of the constitution of 1782—its failure to solve the problem of the relations between the protestant ascendancy and the Roman catholic masses. It was essentially a constitution for the protestant nation. The penal laws, which had been less and less strictly enforced as the century progressed, had been very largely repealed by 1782; but the political disabilities on Roman catholics remained: they could neither sit in parliament nor vote at parliamentary elections. These restrictions were becoming more difficult to maintain. There was an increasing body of protestant opinion in favour of their removal; and among the Roman catholics themselves the nobility and gentry who had survived the penal period and, even more, the growing middle class had begun to take an active interest in politics. Though they had not been allowed to join the volunteers, many of them had given financial support to the movement and had rejoiced at its success. The volunteers in general had supported the removal of restrictions on Roman catholic worship and education; but on the question of political rights they were divided. Flood opposed concession, Grattan supported it; but the latter repeatedly expressed his devotion to the maintenance of a protestant ascendancy, and indeed, as long as parliament continued to represent the landed property of the country there was little danger of its ceasing to be predominantly protestant. The division of opinion on this question among the volunteers was one reason for the decline of their political influence. But the question itself remained active, and the growing dissatisfaction among the Roman catholics proved very useful to political agitators of a different stamp.

The failure to solve the problem of Roman catholic claims was not the only weakness of the constitution of 1782. It failed also in its primary purpose of settling Anglo-Irish relations on a permanently satisfactory basis. The nature of the difficulties to be overcome was imperfectly realised at the time. Neither Grattan nor Flood seems to have understood the importance of the distinction between legislature and executive. They concentrated on securing the legislative independence of the Irish parliament, but they were apparently content to leave government in the hands of an executive over which that parliament had only an indirect and imperfect control. After 1782, as before, Ireland was ruled by a lord lieutenant who exercised very much the same sort of power as a prime minister in England, and who was virtually appointed by and responsible to the British cabinet. He continued to maintain control of parliament, partly by management and partly by corruption, and for the general purposes of administration he could count on the large body of place-men and pensioners to give him a majority. But there were dangerous possibilities in the existence of two formally independent legislatures in a single monarchy. In 1785 their mutual jealousy helped to prevent the conclusion of an Anglo-Irish commercial treaty which would have been to the advantage of both countries. In 1789, when George III had his first fit of insanity, the Irish parliament insisted upon recognising the Prince of Wales as regent of Ireland, before the English parliament had taken corresponding action, and only the king's recovery prevented a constitutional crisis.

In spite of these weaknesses and dangers the constitutional experiment of 1782 might have succeeded but for the French

revolution. For Ireland the effects of this were fatal. All the
elements of unrest were encouraged, and it became more and
more difficult to maintain the authority of government. The
outbreak of war made things worse, for now there was the
danger of French invasion to be faced. To the British government Ireland was the weak point in the line of defence, and the
task of securing it was made more difficult by the existence of
an independent parliament whose claim to represent the Irish
people was being constantly and violently challenged. These
were among the principal factors which led to the legislative union.

In Ireland as in England the outbreak of the French revolution produced a wave of enthusiasm among the supporters of
reform, particularly among the presbyterians of the north,
where the ground had been prepared by the influence of American
ideas. In Belfast the fall of the Bastille was celebrated along with
the battle of the Boyne, and throughout the country the cause of
parliamentary reform was vigorously revived. But the reformers
now included a strong body who could not be satisfied by the
removal of the most glaring abuses of the existing system; they
called for a total sweeping away of the constitution and the
construction, from first principles, of an ideal democratic state.
These changes were most vigorously urged by the societies of
United Irishmen, founded at Belfast and Dublin in 1791 by
Wolfe Tone, a young Dublin barrister, who had been carried
away by the religious and political principles of revolutionary
France. Though the United Irish movement was protestant in its
origins, rationalist in its leadership and radically democratic in its
aims, it derived much of its political importance from its alliance
with Roman catholic leaders, whose claim to political rights it
strongly supported.

This union of hostile forces naturally alarmed parliament
and it was quite ready to support the government in repressive
measures. On the question of concessions to Roman catholics
the position was more complicated. Left to itself, the Irish
administration would have met their claims with unbending resistance; but Pitt hoped to buy their support, and under strong pressure from England an act restoring to them the parliamentary franchise was carried in 1793. This marks a turning-point, for it forced
the portestant ascendancy on to the defensive. The right of Roman
catholics to exercise political power had been recognised, and

there was no longer any logical ground for excluding them from parliament. Even as it was, a reform of the parliamentary system would now give them a great, and perhaps irresistible, influence in the government of the country. The outbreak of the French war in the same year emphasised the danger to the ascendancy. The time for compromise, if there ever had been such a time, was past: the real choice lay between democratic reform and opposition to all reform. The first would lead almost inevitably to republicanism and the separation of Ireland from Great Britain; the second (though as yet only a few people realised it) was to lead straight to legislative union.

The struggle which arose out of these circumstances and disturbed the last decade of the century was not one between Ireland and England, but one between the Irish parliament, representing the property of the kingdom, and a group of radical reformers who wished to make it representative of the whole population and who, to gain their ends, were prepared to use violence at home and to ally themselves with the king's enemies abroad. There was still a liberal parliamentary opposition, led by Grattan, which continued its demand for reform and urged the need to conciliate the Roman catholics by further concessions. But this opposition was out of touch with reality: its remedies took no account of the changed situation brought about by the French revolution, and its most far-reaching concessions would have done little to placate men bent on a complete reconstruction of the state. For an attempt to suppress the United Irishmen had driven the society underground and had brought the extremists into full control of the movement. The most immediate threat to the government came from Ulster. It was here that the United Irishmen were strongest, here that republican ideas borrowed from America and France had taken deepest root, here that men were genuinely filled with a humane enthusiasm which overflowed distinctions of creed and class. But throughout Ireland as a whole there were comparatively few who responded to such leadership, and even in Ulster they were a minority. The economic depression which came with the war stimulated agrarian unrest, always endemic in Ireland, and in the north this took a sectarian character which not only divided Roman catholics from protestants, but churchmen from dissenters. The aggressively protestant Orange societies, which sprang up about 1795, were composed almost exclusively of churchmen and professed a strong loyalty to the crown and constitution; they supplied many recruits to the yeomanry corps raised at this time for the maintenance of order. By 1797 Ireland, and especially Ulster, was in a state of submerged civil war in which political and sectarian differences mutually inflamed one another. The grip which the Irish government had on the situation was a precarious one and it was certain that, if any considerable French force should land, a dangerous and possibly disastrous rebellion would break out.

By this time the leaders of the United Irishmen were determined on violent action and were only awaiting a suitable opportunity. At first they relied upon help from France. But a French expedition of 1796 failed; and after the British naval victory of Camperdown it was hopeless to expect a large invading force. So they resolved to strike without further delay and to trust to their own strength. The whole country had suffered severely under the system of military rule by which the Irish government had tried to crush the revolutionary spirit, and the United Irishmen hoped that the indignation, fear and hatred thus aroused would give vigour to a rebellion. The secret of the conspiracy was ill-kept, the government knew of all that went on, and on the eve of the date fixed for the rising the most important of the leaders were arrested. Lord Edward FitzGerald, an aristocrat turned rebel, brave, enthusiastic, over-sanguine, died from wounds received while resisting arrest. Wolfe Tone himself was in France[1] and only local leaders were available to take charge. The rising broke out on 24 May 1798; six weeks later only a few hunted fugitives remained in arms.

The rebellion was practically confined to the counties of Antrim, Down and Wexford, though there were minor skirmishes in Wicklow and north Leinster. In Antrim and Down some thousands of United Irishmen, mostly presbyterian farmers, turned out with pike and musket; but there was no backbone in the rising and two slight engagements sufficed to scatter them decisively. The fighting in Wexford was much more severe. There, the principles of the United Irishmen and the French revolution counted for little; the driving forces were religion and resentment at military rule. The peasantry, armed for the most part with

1. In 1798, after the rebellion was over, Tone returned to Ireland with an unsuccessful French expedition. He was captured, and committed suicide in prison.

pikes and led by their priests, seized the town of Wexford and
got control of most of the county. But they had no plan of
action, the people of the neighbouring counties did not follow
their example, and there was nothing for them to do but hold out
as long as possible against the ever-increasing forces which the
government brought against them. The courage of their resistance
was only equalled by the ferocity with which they too often
avenged their grievances on those whom they made prisoner.

The significance of the insurrection, brief though it had been,
can hardly be overestimated. It established a tradition of revolutionary violence which, from that time onwards, has exercised
an influence, varying in strength but never negligible, on Irish
politics; and this tradition still contains all those incongruous
elements that were at work in 1798—national feeling, radical
democracy, social discontent, religious fanaticism and humani-
tarian philosophy. In its immediate effects also the rebellion was
of crucial importance. It had thoroughly alarmed not only the
government but the whole protestant ascendancy. They seemed
caught between the old power of Rome, reviving and militant,
on the one hand, and the new danger of radical democracy on the
other. The fear which this double threat aroused goes far to
explain the cruelty with which the Wexford rising was crushed
and leads on directly to the passing of the act of union.

For many years statesmen on both sides of the channel had
considered legislative union a necessity, and the rebellion was a
strong argument in the same direction. In 1798 both adminis-
trations set themselves to prepare the way for it. The main
resistance was naturally in the Irish house of commons. Personal
interest, national pride, a sense of public duty, all combined to
arouse opposition to such a measure. Cornwallis, the lord
lieutenant, Castlereagh, the chief secretary, and Lord Clare,[1] who
had long been one of the leading members of the administration,
threw all their energies into winning a majority, and their efforts
were backed by bribery more extensive than any yet known in the
Irish parliament. A substantial opposition remained to the end,
but though its members voted solidly together against the union,
they were not agreed on any positive policy. Some, led by Grattan,
were ready to make wide concessions to the Roman catholics;
others wished to maintain the existing position. Few of them

1. John Fitzgibbon, first earl of Clare; attorney-general, 1783; lord chancellor,
1789.

seem to have faced the fact that the maintenance of the government's authority now depended directly upon military aid from Britain. If Britain demanded legislative union as a condition of that aid it was useless for them to refuse, unless the refusal were accompanied by some other feasible plan for securing the protestant church and the British connection, to both of which they professed their devotion; but they had no such plan to offer. Outside parliament the resistance to union was badly organised and, in general, unenthusiastic. Fears arising out of the state of Ireland and the state of Europe, and the hopes which the Roman catholics had of getting better terms from a British than from an Irish parliament combined to produce a general inertia. It was the barristers, the Orange societies, and the church of Ireland, all associated with privilege and ascendancy, that provided the backbone of the national resistance.

From the British point of view the union was little short of a military necessity. The second coalition was breaking up and Britain was once more alone in the struggle with France. A restless Ireland was a source of intolerable danger. Ireland conciliated and closely bound to Britain would be a source of strength, especially to the armed forces, for at this time Ireland contained approximately one quarter of the total population of the British Isles. In these circumstances Pitt was naturally anxious that the union should be acceptable to the mass of the people, and he let it be known that in his opinion it should be accompanied by the admission of Roman catholics to membership of parliament, a policy generally known as 'catholic emancipation'. The Roman catholic bishops and landlords, encouraged by this hope, were almost unanimously in favour of union, though their clergy and people gave them little active support, and seem to have been, for the most part, indifferent. But Pitt's first task was to get the union through the Irish house of commons, where the promise of emancipation was not likely to ease its progress, and he did not commit himself definitely by linking the two measures together. To many Irish landlords, indeed, including Lord Clare, the strongest argument in favour of the union was the belief that by no other means could the protestant ascendancy be saved. They accepted it in this spirit, and the act soon came to be regarded as a bulwark of protestantism.

The two identical acts which brought the separate existence of the Irish parliament to an end passed through the parliaments of both kingdoms in 1800 and came into force on 1 January 1801. Henceforth Great Britain and Ireland were to be merged into one 'United Kingdom' with one parliament. In this new parliament Ireland was to be represented by four spiritual and twenty-eight temporal lords in the upper house, and by one hundred members in the lower.[1] There was to be free trade between the two countries, with certain temporary protective duties in favour of Irish goods. The exchequers and national debts were to remain distinct until they could be merged on certain specified terms, which were intended to be just to both sides; this merger did not take place until 1817. The English and Irish churches were to form the 'United Church of England and Ireland', and the maintenance of the ecclesiastical establishment in the two countries was to be 'an essential and fundamental part of the union'. On 2 August 1800 the Irish parliament sat for the last time; on 22 January 1801 the Irish lords and commons took their seats in the first parliament of the United Kingdom of Great Britain and Ireland.

1. In 1832 the numbers of Irish members in the house of commons was increased to 105.

E

5

IRELAND UNDER THE UNION

I. THE NATURE OF THE UNION

The legislative union of Great Britain and Ireland might have been a great measure; but it was conceived in a spirit of expediency and carried through by methods which seriously prejudiced its chance of success. Though it achieved the immediate purpose of strengthening Britain in the struggle against Napoleon, it was in almost every other respect a failure. It was meant to solve finally the problem of Anglo-Irish relations by merging the two kingdoms in one; but in fact this never happened: Ireland retained a separate executive, and over a wide field of legislation was treated as a distinct unit. It was meant to prepare the way for peaceful government; instead, the country had to be ruled under a succession of coercion acts and the problem of maintaining law and order was never solved while the union lasted. It was meant to safeguard the protestant ascendancy; but the British government refused to be bound by the terms of the act of 1800 and having sacrificed the church in the hope of saving the land-lords, then bought out the landlords in the hope of saving the union. This was a vain policy, which destroyed the power of a protestant ascendancy, bound by every tie to the British connection, only to replace it by a Roman catholic democracy strongly inclined to seek complete independence.

The basic failure of the act of union appears in the continued existence of a separate Irish executive. The legislature had been removed to Westminster, but the lord lieutenant, the council and the law-courts remained in Dublin, and the 'Castle' continued to be the real centre of Irish government. In the long run, of course, this government was responsible to parliament, and changes in party fortune at Westminster produced corresponding changes in Dublin; but for more than thirty years after 1800 the spirit of the Irish administration remained essentially that of the pre-union ascendancy, and while the union lasted the ascendancy influence was never wholly eradicated. It might be argued that the maintenance of a separate executive was a necessary part of the implied bargain by which the Irish landlord class had surrendered its control over the legislature in return for a guarantee of the protestant ascendancy, which, we must in fairness add, it identified with law and order and the rights of property. Since Ireland was to be governed in the interests of a minority the Irish executive must be on a different footing from the English. But though this executive was almost universally regarded as an instrument of the protestant ascendancy, it was also a constant reminder of Ireland's former independence. For this reason it was valued even by many of those who hated its policy: O'Connell, for example, though a bitter opponent of almost every Irish government of his time, was strongly opposed to any suggestion that the office of lord lieutenant should be abolished.

The existence of this system of Irish government helps to account for the inconsistent attitude of British statesmen towards Irish affairs. They regarded Ireland sometimes as an integral part of the kingdom and sometimes as a dependency. They could speak, for example, of '*our* duty to Ireland', thus distinguishing in their minds between Great Britain as one entity and Ireland as another. But the suggestion that this mental distinction should be turned into a legislative one shocked them. In order to understand the history of nineteenth-century Ireland it is necessary to take this paradox into full account. It arose from a factor in the situation which is sometimes overlooked and sometimes misrepresented—English nationalism. For the British statesman, and for the British public, the union of 1800 had completed a natural process by which a single system of government was extended over the whole British Isles. Regional distinctions had for all practical political purposes disappeared and there was one British nation. This nation had the English monarchy and parliamentary system for its centre, English was its official and almost universal language, English wealth the main basis of its power. It was not surprising that the Englishman should come

to regard the terms 'British' and 'English' as almost interchangeable. It was natural also that he should regard any attempt
to break up this national unity not as a legitimate desire for self-
government, such as he was prepared to approve in South
America or Greece or Belgium, but as treason against the nation.

The uncertainty of British statesmen's attitude towards Ireland
was intensified by their ignorance of the country. It was not
ignorance of matters of fact, for the government was indefatigable
in collecting information and publishing reports on almost every
aspect of life—agriculture, fisheries, manufactures, population,
health, education, bogs, railways, canals; it was ignorance of the
country itself, of the people and their ways of thought. Gladstone,
for example, despite his long interest in Irish affairs, visited Ireland
only once and stayed less than a month. This ignorance, which was
almost universal among the British ruling class, undoubtedly
strengthened the tendency to regard Ireland as a half-alien
dependency. Even so scrupulous a politician as Acton sat in
parliament for an Irish pocket borough without showing any
sense of obligation either towards his constituents or towards
Ireland as a whole.

The incompleteness of the constitutional union between the
two countries was perhaps a symptom rather than a cause of
Ireland's political unhealthiness. It was less obvious, but in some
ways more important, that the economic union was also incomplete, in spite of the amalgamation in 1817 of the financial
systems and the removal in 1825 of the temporary protection given
to Irish manufactures against British competition. Ireland was
brought into the richest community in the world, but she had
little share in the surplus capital of Great Britain. Some contemporaries blamed the disturbed state of the country for the fact
that British industrialists showed little inclination to invest money
in Ireland; but they invested freely in the republics of Central
and South America, where the security was certainly no greater.
Economically, Ireland had to suffer many of the disadvantages
of being linked with a wealthy partner without enjoying the
corresponding benefits. The lack of capital affected every aspect
of Irish social life and had inevitable repercussions on politics.
It is true that in some respects the early years of the nineteenth
century saw an improvement in the economic situation. The total
volume of trade increased, the price of corn continued to rise and

there was an expanding market for Irish provisions. But the advantage to Ireland of this improvement was partly illusory, for a steady increase in rents brought the bulk of the additional profit into the hands of the landlords, who spent a great part of it abroad. In another way also Irish money was being drained into England. Ireland's share of the heavy war expenses had had to be met largely by loans raised in England, and the interest drew off a dangerously high proportion of the national income. This process was to some extent modified by the amalgamation of the exchequers in 1817, but it remained true that in so far as any flow of capital was stimulated by the union it was a flow away from Ireland.

The continued and rapid increase in the population made the lack of capital particularly dangerous. Ireland had between four and five million inhabitants in 1801, almost seven million in 1821, over eight million in 1841. Except in the north there was almost no source of livelihood but the land, and it could not bear this constantly increasing pressure. Estates and farms were subdivided into a multitude of holdings so small that they could never be worked economically. The peasant's standard of living sank even lower than before, and the margin which divided him from actual starvation became very narrow indeed. In these circumstances the establishment of peasant proprietorship, even if it had been politically possible, would have produced little permanent improvement. The root of the evil lay elsewhere. As the *Quarterly Review*[1] put it, 'The curse of Ireland is the general want of employment for its inhabitants.' If there had been a steady flow of capital to provide this, the land problem would have virtually disappeared. Rents would have fallen to an economic level; estates could have been cleared and holdings consolidated without throwing those evicted out of all employment; above all, the landlord's monopoly of the means of livelihood having been taken away his social and political influence would have tended to decline, and ill-feeling between landlord and tenant would have gradually diminished.

The nature of this economic problem was fairly widely recog-nised among those British economists and politicians who paid any attention to Irish affairs; but the dominant political philo-sophy of the day forbade the government to take any action. In 1836 a committee appointed by Lord Grey to consider the

1. January 1832.

relief of poverty in Ireland recommended a scheme of public works; a few years later a royal commission on railways recommended a national system and pointed out the benefit to the whole community of the additional employment thus to be provided. But both reports were passed over. The English poor law system was extended to Ireland in 1838, and the development of Irish railways was left, for the time being, to private enterprise. The argument of the *Edinburgh Review*[1] prevailed, that if the capitalists of the country could not provide work it was impracticable for the state to attempt to do so. In this and other respects Ireland suffered from the application of *laissez-faire* principles, which, however successful they might be in Britain, were ill-suited to the circumstances in Ireland. The establishment of free trade, for example, was almost as damaging to many Irish manufactures in the nineteenth century as English protectionism had been in the eighteenth; and the peasantry suffered under legislation designed to simplify the process of eviction, so that landlords might manage their estates more efficiently by getting rid of impoverished tenants.

British mishandling of Irish affairs arose largely from ignorance and neglect. But even for the best-intentioned of statesmen the task of dealing justly with Ireland was infinitely complicated by the intermixture of economic and political problems. The landlords represented not only a social class but a political system—the continuing protestant ascendancy. They had accepted the union, reluctantly, as the only means of safeguarding their privileged position and they were determined to maintain it to the same end. The whole local administration of the country was in their hands. They controlled the magistracy, the police, the grand juries and the municipal corporations. The removal of political disabilities on Roman catholics in 1829 only partly altered this state of affairs; even the reform of the municipal corporations in 1840 did not bring their control to an end, and it seemed almost impossible to govern without their co-operation. The policy of the ascendancy party was to claim a monopoly of 'loyalty' and to identify agrarian outrages with acts of rebellion. But the endemic disorder of which they complained, and which made normal methods of government unworkable, was the natural result of the economic situation. On the face of it, the

1. October 1837.

landlords could make out a good case for strong government support; all they wanted to do was to enforce the law, protect the rights of property and keep the country quiet. In response to every fresh disturbance they demanded, and usually obtained, sterner measures of repression; for more than twenty years after the union Ireland was governed under a series of coercion acts which suspended the normal safeguards of individual liberty. But such a system could not bring permanent peace while there was so much bitter poverty and while the courts were in the hands of the very people generally held responsible for it. Rack rents and tithes were not the root causes of Ireland's distress, but they were the two forms in which it most closely touched the peasantry, and both were looked upon as the unjust impositions of the protestant ascendancy. No policy which ignored them would satisfy the mass of the people; any attempt to interfere with them would arouse the opposition of the church and the landlords and of their powerful allies in England.

The landlords were not alone in their support of the union and their demand for strong government. They had the backing of almost the whole protestant population. It was natural enough that the established church, however suspicious of the union to begin with, should speedily accept a settlement which seemed to guarantee its position, but the attitude of the Ulster presbyterians calls for some comment. They did not immediately or unanimously abandon the liberal and nationalist outlook which had characterised them at the end of the eighteenth century; and for twenty years after the union the government remained suspicious of their loyalty, though perhaps without much cause. But fear of the Roman catholics combined with the rapidly increasing economic prosperity of the north-eastern counties to convince them that their welfare was bound up with the maintenance of the union. Relations between landlord and tenant were already much better in Ulster than elsewhere, and even the long-standing jealousy between the presbyterians and the church of Ireland was gradually broken down by the fear of a common enemy, a fear which was decisively stimulated by the new nationalism expounded by Daniel O'Connell.[1] The dominant industrial position later attained by the Belfast area made this conversion of Ulster to the cause of union one of the most significant events in modern Irish history.

1. See below.

The legislative union was established in the interests of Great Britain and in some ways served those interests well; but its failure to bring about a genuine incorporation of the two countries had a profound and almost disastrous effect on British political life. Irish problems remained distinct; but now they had to be thrashed out in the imperial parliament, where they often exercised a decisive influence and consumed a disproportionate amount of parliamentary time. The growth of a strong Irish party upset the political balance: relations between the two great British parties were embittered, and a disruptive element was introduced within the parties themselves. From the time of Parnell onwards the situation became increasingly dangerous, and if the union had not been dissolved it is hard to see how parliamentary government and the party system could have survived in Britain.

2. THE NEW NATIONALISM

The aristocratic nationalism of the volunteers and the revolutionary nationalism of the United Irishmen were both in rapid decay at the time of the union. A sentimental regret for the glories of the Irish parliament lingered for a while among the ascendancy class, and the United Irish spirit left a brief postscript in Robert Emmet's abortive insurrection of 1803. But for many years after the union Ireland as a whole was politically stagnant. The secret societies which existed in many parts of the country— Whitefeet, Blackfeet, Shanavests, Rockites—were not engaged in a national struggle, but in local class warfare against the landlords and against the tithe-proctors who acted for the clergy of the established church. There was all the material for a powerful political movement, but to begin with there was neither a great cause nor a great leader to unite all the various groups and inspire them with the enthusiasm of a common effort. It was the work of Daniel O'Connell to bring about this union, and in doing so he linked the cause of Irish nationalism and the cause of the Roman catholic church so firmly together that succeeding generations have hardly been able to prise them apart.

Such a linking-up was perhaps the only means of providing the feeling of solidarity without which an Irish popular movement could hardly have emerged. There was no general sentiment against the union. The grievances of the peasantry were strongly

felt and sometimes savagely avenged, but the organisation of a
land war on a national scale would have required a degree of co-
operation and leadership which the peasantry could not supply
for themselves and which, in the intellectual atmosphere of the
early nineteenth century, they were not likely to get from any other
class. The one issue round which it might be possible to build up
a strong party was the demand for 'catholic emancipation', i.e.
the removal of the remaining political restrictions on Roman
catholics, and especially those excluding them from membership
of parliament. Pitt had hoped to carry this through immediately
after the union, but the opposition was stronger than he had
expected, the measure had to be dropped and he resigned in
protest. The Irish Roman catholics were bitterly disappointed,
but it was some time before the political possibilities of this
disappointment were fully exploited. Their case was organised
for the most part by noblemen and gentry who had a great
respect for constitutional authority and a great fear of revolution.
They had the support of many members of parliament, both
English and Irish, among whom Grattan was perhaps their most
faithful advocate. But even Grattan believed that emancipation
was quite consistent with the maintenance of the protestant
ascendancy and that the influence of property would always
outweigh the influence of numbers. With such leaders and such
allies the Roman catholics were prepared to follow the most
moderate methods and accept the most moderate concessions.

The advent of O'Connell changed the whole situation. He was a
brilliantly successful barrister, who specialised in criminal cases,
and apart altogether from his political activities he had won
fame and popularity among the mass of the people, who were
inclined to regard every successful defence as a victory over the
government. As a young man O'Connell had used such influence
as he possessed against the act of union and he never ceased to
condemn it. At least as early as 1811 he had given public support
to the proposal for its repeal; but repeal was not yet a practicable
policy, and so he threw himself into the struggle for emancipation
with the determination that it should lead to a popular victory,
won for and by the masses. With this end in view he strongly
opposed a compromise settlement, discussed between 1813 and
1815, by which the government would have been given a veto in
episcopal elections in return for the admission of Roman catholics
to parliament. Though this proposal had the support of the

Vatican, it was absolutely rejected by the Irish Roman catholic
bishops, largely under O'Connell's influence.

There can be no doubt that O'Connell acted on a true instinct.
A church which was even suspected of being the agent of the
British government could never have become the main unifying
influence in the new nation he was trying to create. But the veto
question divided the ranks of those who supported emancipation
and undoubtedly delayed their success. This very delay, however,
left the way open for O'Connell to establish unrivalled supremacy
in the movement. After a period of sporadic and fruitless effort
the Catholic Association had been founded in 1823 to press the
case more actively, and though it included a number of peers and
other landlords it was predominantly a popular body. The parish
was its unit of organisation and its local agents were the parish
priests. It was they who collected the 'catholic rent', a sub-
scription of a penny a month which provided the association
with its campaigning fund, and their political influence over their
people soon came to outweigh even the traditional supremacy
of the landlord. The Catholic Association was the instrument by
which O'Connell established and maintained his control of the
movement. He had been chiefly responsible for calling the
clergy into the struggle and he could count on their support.
The immense resources of the 'catholic rent' were at his absolute
disposal. Against the mounting pressure of O'Connell's agitation
in Ireland the British government offered a very uncertain front.
Though Peel and Wellington had come into office in 1828 pledged
to resist the Roman catholic demands, their position in the house
of commons was precarious, and it was by no means certain that
they would be able to secure support for the additional coercive
measures that would be necessary if emancipation were longer
withheld. In these circumstances they decided to give way, and
in 1829 parliament was opened to Roman catholics.

The methods by which O'Connell achieved his success were
no less significant than the success itself. Before his time the
Roman catholic movement was a middle-class one, under
aristocratic leadership. He changed its whole character by
bringing in the clergy and the peasantry. By his system of organisation, by his persistent propaganda, above all, perhaps, by the
great public meetings which gave full opportunity to his unrivalled
powers of oratory, he used the cause of emancipation to inspire
the Roman catholic masses with a sense of united purpose such

as they had never known before. He was a pioneer in bringing
the force of public opinion to bear on government in a constitutional and yet aggressive way; his achievement attracted a
great deal of attention outside Ireland and his example was
followed both in Britain and on the continent.

The admission of Roman catholics to parliament placed a
new weapon in O'Connell's hands. He built up a parliamentary
party of his own and for a time held the balance of power in the
house of commons. Naturally, he was inclined to support the
whigs, and in 1835 made a limited alliance with them, which
enabled Melbourne to take office. The whigs were well disposed
towards Ireland, but they were themselves divided on the best
policy to follow. The division was deepest on the church question,
which was, after emancipation had been granted, the most
controversial in Irish politics. The English and Irish churches
had been united by the act of 1800 and their security had been
guaranteed afresh in the emancipation act. But the union was
no more than nominal, public opinion in general regarded the
Irish establishment as resting on a very different basis from
the English, and the defence of the former was not, as Irish
churchmen had expected, made part and parcel of the defence of
the latter. The line of attack which O'Connell now particularly
pressed was one with which many English whigs were inclined
to sympathise. He denounced the tithe system as not only oppressive in itself, but as especially hateful to the Roman catholic
peasantry, who were compelled to contribute to the upkeep of a
church which they regarded as alien and heretical. It was an old
dispute, which became particularly bitter in the 1830s; and,
though O'Connell himself lent no countenance to violence, great
parts of the country were convulsed by a 'tithe war', and many of
the established clergy were reduced to poverty by the impossibility
of collecting their dues. The whigs were prepared to alter the
methods of assessment and collection so as to ease the burden
on the tenantry, but they were held back from more drastic
action by their own respect for the rights of property and the
peers' respect for the rights of the church. So the tithe charge
remained, in a somewhat modified form, and the revenue from
it was not, as O'Connell and some of the English whigs desired,
diverted to secular purposes. As a further concession to critics
of the established church ten bishoprics were suppressed and their
property applied to other ecclesiastical purposes. But though this

strong assertion of parliamentary authority may be regarded as a step towards disestablishment, it was not in itself likely to conciliate Roman catholic opinion.

This half-hearted attack on the church question was characteristic of the whigs' policy in Ireland. Urged on by O'Connell to more radical reforms, restrained by the cautious among themselves, exposed to constant attack by an aggressive opposition in the commons and hampered by the steady resistance of the house of lords, they moved from expedient to expedient, without any fixed purpose beyond the evasion of the immediate problem. But, in spite of their fumbling, they did accomplish something. They set up a national system of elementary education, they extended the new English poor law to Ireland and they reformed the municipal corporations. The wisdom of these measures may be disputed, but all of them were significant. The national schools failed to realise their original purpose of bringing together children of different religious denominations, but they raised the standard of literacy, and their influence, together with that of O'Connell and the Roman catholic church, went far towards destroying Irish as a spoken language. The new poor law was almost entirely unsuited to Irish conditions, but it was at least a line of defence against absolute starvation. The reform of the municipal corporations was a first step towards transferring control of local government to the Roman catholic majority. Against the whigs' failure to produce a consistent Irish policy must be set the fact that they made a notable, though temporary, change in the administration. Between 1835 and 1840 the ascendancy spirit had to give way to the liberalism of the under-secretary, Thomas Drummond. Stipendiary magistrates were appointed in large numbers to balance the influence of the landlords, Orange processions were forbidden, the control of the police was brought more firmly into the hands of the government and a larger proportion of public appointments was given to Roman catholics.

The whole tendency of Drummond's policy was to bring more and more power into the hands of government officials and to undermine the influence of the protestant gentry. With this O'Connell was well enough satisfied, especially as his opinion was given great weight in the making of appointments; but in general he was disappointed with the results of the whig alliance, and in 1840 he prepared to bring it to an end. He was strongly

influenced in this direction by the fact that Melbourne's government was obviously on the point of collapse. Peel's turn was
about to come at last, and with Peel he could have no sort of
understanding. Instead, he founded the Repeal Association in
1840 and renewed the policy of agitation with all the old violence.
O'Connell has been strongly criticised for his conduct at this
point. He has been accused of reviving repeal in order to bolster
up his declining influence in the country, or even for the sake of
financial advantage. It is certainly true that his power was much
less than it had been at the height of the struggle for emancipation, and that the 'tribute' (a levy which had taken the place
of the 'catholic rent' and which supplied him with his political
funds) had seriously declined. It is true also that O'Connell was
fond of the exercise of power, and so carelessly extravagant in
his expenditure as to be continuously short of money. But, though
the revival of the repeal agitation might in this way suit his own
purposes, his devotion to the cause was genuine, and the political
circumstances provide a perfectly adequate explanation of his
conduct. There are, however, two more valid grounds of criticism. In the first place, O'Connell concentrated on constitutional
and not on social issues. This was perhaps the natural result of
his training and his environment, but a greater man might have
seen that in the Ireland of the 1840s a purely political programme
could accomplish little. Secondly, even on the political level he
showed a lack of insight. In 1829 Peel and Wellington had yielded
to his demand for emancipation not merely because of the state
of Ireland, but because of the division of opinion in Britain.
In the 1840s British opinion was solidly in favour of maintaining
the union, Peel's parliamentary majority was secure, and he
could safely take such measures as he thought necessary to
maintain order in Ireland. O'Connell hoped to frighten him by
'peaceful, legal and constitutional' agitation. He had not considered what would happen if the agitation failed.

The repeal agitation thus launched upon its new career was
intended by O'Connell to be a national movement. But, despite
his protestations and his efforts, its supporters were almost
exclusively Roman catholics. He had hoped to win over the
presbyterians of the north, but in this he miscalculated almost
as seriously as in his estimate of Peel's power of resistance. His
own policy of close alliance with and dependence upon the
Roman catholic clergy had alarmed and alienated almost the

last remnants of presbyterian nationalism, and though he came
to Belfast it was to address a meeting of his co-religionists. The
spirit now dominant among the presbyterians found its strongest
expression in the speeches of one of their ministers, Henry Cooke,
an orator not altogether unworthy of comparison with O'Connell
himself, and in power of invective perhaps even his equal. Under
Cooke's guidance the presbyterians definitely ranged themselves
beside the established church in defence of the union. There
were indeed many protestants who joined the Repeal Association,
and some who played an important part in it, but they were not
representative of any considerable body of protestant opinion.
Modern Irish nationalism, in so far as it springs from O'Connell,
is distinctively, almost essentially, Roman catholic.

The outstanding victory which O'Connell had won in 1829 led
him and his supporters to expect another success for the same
methods of agitation. But Peel refused to be intimidated.
O'Connell had virtually defied the government to prohibit the
monster meetings which he was holding throughout the country,
and the government took up the challenge. A meeting arranged
for Clontarf in October 1843 was proclaimed on the eve of the
appointed date. O'Connell cancelled it at once and by the exercise
of his great influence prevented any kind of disturbance. This was
the sensible thing to do and was strictly in accordance with his
well-known determination to avoid violence, but nevertheless the
surrender was a shock to his prestige from which he never
recovered. From this time onwards, also, he himself seemed to
lose faith in the method of agitation, and even in the cause of
repeal, and to look forward to future co-operation with the whigs
when they should return to office.

The set-back for O'Connell was of the greater importance
because his whole line of policy was at this time being challenged,
actually though not yet openly, by a nationalist movement of
another stamp. The ideas of 'ninety-eight' were in the air again
and were being taken up by a group of enthusiasts (generally
known as 'Young Ireland') who were members of the Repeal
Association, but who were also strongly influenced by the
revolutionary tradition of contemporary Europe. The Young
Ireland leaders had great reverence for O'Connell, as well they
might, for it was he who had aroused the popular feeling which
they hoped to educate, and they were anxious to work under
him; but they had little patience with his determined opposition

to the use of force and none at all with his clericalism. They were drawn partly from the protestant middle class, and looked for an Ireland in which men of all faiths would mingle freely; and they were willing, it seemed at times almost anxious, that it should be won by a people in arms. Their newspaper, the *Nation*, glorified the military achievements of the past and advocated military training in the present. After a good deal of suspicion and uneasiness on both sides the first open quarrel between O'Connell and the Young Irelanders came in 1845, and it is significant that it was on a religious issue. In that year Peel's government established three 'Queen's Colleges', at Belfast, Cork and Galway, to meet the need for university education in Ireland. The colleges were to be undenominational and were intended to bring together students of all creeds; O'Connell joined the Roman catholic bishops in denouncing them as 'godless' and in condemning the policy of 'mixed education', a policy which the Young Irelanders, especially Thomas Davis, enthusiastically supported. The quarrel was followed by a formal reconciliation; but O'Connell and the bishops had their way. The Queen's Colleges of Cork and Galway, which depended on a predominantly Roman catholic population, languished for over half a century; the college at Belfast, being accepted by the presbyterian community, had a rather happier history. The whole dispute revealed the essentially clerical character of O'Connell's nationalism, and the difference between his outlook and that of the Young Irelanders was too deep to be glossed over. In 1846 they were compelled to leave the association; and though the occasion of the separation was their refusal to renounce completely the use of physical force, this was only one aspect of a fundamental divergence. In the whole affair there was no doubt some element of personal jealousy, for an old leader can rarely endure to have his authority questioned by a new generation. But this merely strengthened the contrast between a constitutional movement backed by the church, on the one hand, and a secular and revolutionary movement on the other.

The political pattern of the 1840s was to be repeated more than half a century later, when once again a physical force party grew up within a constitutional movement and split off from it, though this time with very different results. But despite the vigorous re-emergence of the violent and revolutionary policy which he hated, it was O'Connell who gave to modern Irish nationalism its distinctive characteristics as a popular and largely

clerical movement. The victories won by a revolutionary minority
have only enabled it to realise these characteristics more fully.

The quarrel between O'Connell and the Young Irelanders
was almost completely overshadowed by the great tragedy of
the famine. The population had risen to over 8,000,000, about
half of whom existed almost wholly on potatoes. It was a precarious state of affairs: a partial failure of the crop in 1816 had
nearly produced a disaster, and the fact that fever was endemic
throughout the country threatened plague conditions if resistance
to infection were reduced by shortage of food. Informed opinion
had long been aware that the economy of Ireland was dangerously
unbalanced; but no government of the period was prepared to
tackle such a vast economic problem, and anyhow it was impossible to foresee a disaster of the magnitude which actually
occurred or to take adequate measures against it. The famine
began with a partial failure of the potato crop in the autumn of
1845, it reached its height during 1846 and 1847, by 1848 the
worst was over. During these four years Ireland had lost, by death
and emigration, over 1,000,000 of her people; in 1847 alone it is
reckoned that almost 250,000 died of starvation or fever and over
200,000 fled to America.

The famine faced the government with an almost insoluble
problem of administration. There was a serious shortage of food
in Britain, which made it politically impossible to prohibit the
export of grain from Ireland, and the opening of the ports to
foreign supplies by repeal of the corn laws came too late to have
much effect. Besides, the problem in Ireland was not merely one
of food supply. The Irish peasant lived mainly on the potatoes he
grew himself, and when they failed he had no money to buy
anything in their place. The attempt to meet the situation by
establishing public works led to jobbery and mismanagement,
and in the end the government had to arrange for outdoor relief
on a gigantic scale. The efforts of the government were backed
up by voluntary assistance from almost all parts of the world,
and in the spring of 1847 some 3,000,000 people were being
supported by public funds. Though their sufferings were in-
comparably lighter, and their claim on public compassion by no
means so obvious, landlords as well as peasants felt the ill-effects
of the famine. Many of them sacrificed their fortunes in an effort
to save their tenantry; but others insisted on their rights, and in

some areas wholesale evictions added to the miseries of famine
and disease.

The influence of the famine was so tremendous that it touched
almost every department of life. Its most spectacular result was
a rapid and permanent decline in the population, to six and a half
million in 1851 and five and a half million in 1871. This decline
affected mainly the rural areas, but it did not immediately
improve the position of the peasantry; for after the famine the
consolidation of holdings continued fairly rapidly, so that the
competition for land was almost as severe as before. But within
forty years the population had sunk to a level which Ireland's
agricultural economy could safely support, and a system of
peasant proprietorship, which would have been impracticable
in the first half of the century, was now the obvious solution to
the land problem. The famine had also more direct and immediate effects on the course of politics. It killed the organised
movement for repeal. 'The high aspirations after a national
senate and a national flag had sunk to a mere craving for food':
so wrote John Mitchel, the most violent of the Young Ireland
party and an opponent of O'Connell's policy of constitutional
agitation. The Young Irelanders' own attempt at revolution, in
1848, was a mere fiasco, for the exhaustion which followed the
famine produced general apathy on political issues. But the
nationalist spirit raised by O'Connell was not dead, and in its
recovery it was embittered by the conviction that the British
government was in some way responsible, if not for the famine
itself, at least for its magnitude. The steady stream of emigration,
which persisted for decades, also affected the political position.
It established in the United States a huge Irish population whose
sense of national solidarity was based mainly on hatred of
Britain, and it was among the American Irish that the tradition
of violent revolution was most active. The general tendency of
these political influences was to widen the already existing gap
between Ulster and the rest of Ireland. The population there
depended less completely on the potato and so suffered less
severely from its failure than the population of the other provinces; the memory of 'black forty-seven' plays little part in
Ulster tradition. Besides this, Ulster industries continued to
expand, while those of the south and west, already suffering from
English competition, declined more rapidly than ever. In the new

Ireland which gradually emerged from the chaos of the famine years the distinctive character of the north-eastern counties was even more sharply marked than before.

3. THE POLICY OF HOME RULE

The famine left Ireland politically as well as economically exhausted. The movement for repeal was dead; the Young Irelanders were scattered and discredited; no leader came forward to take O'Connell's place; Ireland had no national party and the British government had no Irish policy. Forty years later all was changed. Parnell enjoyed a supremacy no less striking, though less securely based, than that of O'Connell, and he had behind him a well-disciplined parliamentary party which comprised over eighty per cent of the Irish representation at Westminster. Instead of repeal the Irish nationalists now demanded a separate, though dependent, Irish parliament, and this policy of 'home rule' had been officially adopted by one of the two great British parties. The hope which these circumstances naturally inspired was not fulfilled. Pressure of Irish opinion secured many social reforms, but not a constitutional settlement of the political problem. This long-drawn-out failure opened the way for more vigorous and more revolutionary leadership in nationalist Ireland, and the home rule movement collapsed, having all but destroyed the British parliamentary system, and dragging down with it the fortunes of the Liberal party.

The course of Irish politics in the latter half of the nineteenth century can be traced directly to the government's attitude in the years after the famine. British sympathy and interest, aroused by that disaster, had soon died down again and there was no essential change in either the policy or the spirit of the administration. Yet some such change was urgently required, for Ireland was entering upon a new era. The sudden decline in population was the most striking, but not the only, indication of this; there was also a shifting of the balance in the structure of rural society. The cottier class almost disappeared: between the census of 1841 and that of 1851 the number of one-roomed cabins had declined by seventy per cent, while during the same period the number of holdings of over fifteen acres had almost doubled. This apparent improvement was offset by other factors. The repeal of the corn laws led to a fall in the price of grain—in Ireland it fell by over twenty-five per cent between 1840 and 1850—and thus the small farmer's earning-power was reduced. But rents did not fall accordingly, and the rise in the price of cattle during the same period was a further inducement to landlords to clear their estates and let them out in large grazing farms, with the natural result that the demand for labour declined. Agricultural wages, which had risen somewhat immediately after the famine, remained almost static for a long time, though there was a general rise in the cost of living. So many small farmers depended upon increasing their scanty profits by occasional labour that this state of under-employment and low wages was a serious hardship to a large section of the tenantry.

It was not to be expected that the government would realise fully the significance of the changes that were coming over Irish life, though the famine should have made it clear that the situation required special legislation. But during the 1850s and early 1860s the *laissez-faire* attitude of the period, which would in any case have made it difficult for the government to interfere with economic processes, was reinforced by the absorbing interest of foreign affairs. With the Crimean war, the Indian mutiny and the liberation of Italy to occupy their attention, neither the people nor the government of Britain had time for Ireland; special legislation was indeed provided, but it dealt with the symptoms, not the causes, of unrest. Agrarian crime, always endemic in Ireland, had increased during the chaos of the famine and the insecurity of the period which followed. Between 1847 and 1857 parliament passed twelve coercion acts giving the executive special powers and suspending the normal liberties of the subject. For a more permanent solution of the problem Englishmen were inclined to trust to the effect produced by the steady decline of the population.

Though English public opinion was thus prepared to let things take their course, there was some effort in Ireland to force the government into constructive action. Many local organisations had been formed for the protection of tenants, and in 1850 these were grouped together in the Irish Tenant Right League, the so-called 'League of north and south'. This was significant as an attempt to combine Roman catholics and protestants in a common cause, but even more significant as an experiment in using the land agitation as the basis of a national party. The

League had considerable, but short-lived, success. At the general election of 1852 about forty of its nominees were returned to parliament, pledged to stand together as an independent Irish party and secure the passage of a land bill guaranteeing tenant farmers a greater degree of security in their holdings. But though united on the land question the party was liable to split on religion, whicht he re-establishment of a papal hierarchy in England and the consequent 'no popery' agitation had once more made a live issue in British politics. Most of the Irish Roman catholic bishops were more concerned about this than about tenant right, which Archbishop Cullen, in particular, looked upon with suspicion as an attack upon property. The party so far stuck to its principles as to reject a government measure which offered only part of what it was fighting for, but a few months later two of its most prominent leaders, despite their election pledges, accepted government office, and the Tenant Right League was hopelessly and ignominiously shattered.

After this failure Irish politics entered upon a period of stagnation. A small parliamentary group maintained for a time the struggle for land reform, but the idea of a constitutional movement on a national scale had received a set-back from which it did not recover for almost twenty years. Economically also, the outlook seemed hopeless, except in the north-east, where the Belfast industrial area was advancing rapidly in wealth and population. Elsewhere, the slight recovery which had followed the famine was checked by a series of unfavourable seasons beginning in 1859. Between 1860 and 1870, while the population was still falling rapidly the number of those seeking poor relief increased by seventy-five per cent. Evictions continued unchecked, and the peasantry, as usual, sought protection in secret societies and organised crime, which provided at least superficial justification for the government's repressive policy. The period of political stagnation ended in the 1860s, and the first indication of the change was an ineffective effort at violent revolution.

The Irish Republican Brotherhood, which formed the core of what is usually called the 'fenian' movement, was founded in 1858, but it was some years before it showed much activity. It professed to exercise authority in the name of the Irish republic, 'now virtually established', and was opposed to constitutional methods or a compromise settlement. The movement was strongest among the Irish exiles in the United States, but was

established also in South Africa and Australia, and among the
Irish colonies in Great Britain. In Ireland itself it was consistently
opposed by the Roman catholic church and there was little in its
programme to appeal to the tenant farmer or the agricultural
labourer; though it had some thousands of supporters it was
never in any sense a popular movement. Attempts at insurrection
in 1867 came to nothing, and thereafter fenianism in Ireland
steadily declined. But even in failure it exercised a considerable
indirect influence on Irish opinion, and it served to remind
British statesmen that there was an Irish problem to be solved.
The republican tradition, though forced into the background by
its own deficiencies and by the revival of the constitutional
movement, did not disappear. It still had wide support among
Irish-Americans and through them it reacted in later years on a
nationalist Ireland which had grown tired of oratorical politics
and parliamentary manœuvre.

The influence of fenianism on British policy appears most
clearly in the career of Gladstone. He himself had long been
uneasy about the state of Ireland; but it was not until fenian
activity had aroused public concern in Britain that he openly
took up the 'Irish question'; and in 1868 he entered upon his first
ministry with the famous declaration: 'My mission is to pacify
Ireland'. His first step in that direction was to disestablish and
disendow the Irish church; this removed one of the standing
grievances of the majority, and though it aroused bitter resentment among churchmen, it was in the main healthy for the church
herself. Gladstone's next measure was the land act of 1870, a
rather timid attack upon the problem, which did very little for the
tenants, but which at least established the principle, hitherto
almost completely ignored, that the government had some responsibility for their welfare. In later years Gladstone's Irish
policy was to be, in appearance, much more adventurous, but the
vital decision was taken in this first ministry. By his summary
treatment of the church and his cautious, but significant, attempt
to limit the authority of the landlords he was in effect destroying
the basis upon which the parliamentary union had been set up
and upon which it had so far been maintained. His policy was a
confession that that basis was insecure, but subsequent experiment failed to establish any more durable substitute.

In Ireland as in England the fenian movement had a strong
effect upon the course of politics, and by a kind of reaction

150 *A short history of Ireland*

helped to bring about the establishment of a new Irish parliamentary party. The Home Government Association, which soon became the Home Rule League, was founded in 1870 by Isaac Butt, a protestant barrister who had been professor of political economy in Trinity College, Dublin. He had at one time been a strong Conservative and he hoped to unite Conservatives and Liberals, Roman catholics and protestants, in his new movement. To begin with, indeed, it was not strictly 'nationalist' at all. Butt maintained that in existing circumstances Ireland required special treatment, and that this could be most conveniently provided for by the establishment of an Irish parliament, subordinate to that at Westminster, to manage purely Irish affairs. Such a scheme implied a degree of understanding and good will which did not exist on either side. Butt's spirit of moderation was not widely shared by his followers, and most Irishmen who supported home rule did so out of bitter hostility to English domination in Ireland; and Englishmen in general opposed it as involving the dissolution of the union and the disintegration of the empire. The policy of home rule, no matter how it might be limited in official pronouncements, soon came to be identified on all sides with the demand for national self-government. This strengthened its appeal in Ireland, where the nationalist spirit was reviving, and the problem of conciliating English opinion did not at first arise. In the general election of 1874, the first to be held by secret ballot, almost sixty home-rulers were returned. They at once resolved to stand together as an independent Irish party, to press the demand for home rule, and to ally with neither government nor opposition. The formation of such a party, and a party comprising a majority of the Irish members, was a considerable achievement. As Butt put it: 'The foundation is laid for great results if we wisely and at the same time boldly use the vantage ground we have gained.' He himself, however, favoured 'wisdom' rather than 'boldness' and he made little practical use of the parliamentary party which he had created. This moderation cost him his position when a vigorous rival appeared. In 1875 Charles Stewart Parnell entered parliament as a home-ruler and within a few years he had ousted Butt from effective leadership. Parnell was a protestant landlord, of an old and distinguished Anglo-Irish family. The chief element in his patriotism was hatred of England, learnt from his American mother, and the driving-force in his political life was love of power. Butt had tried to persuade

the English by reasoned argument that Ireland should be allowed
to govern herself; Parnell set out to compel them to surrender by
making the existing system unworkable. He adopted and extended
the method of organised obstruction which almost brought the
business of parliament to a stand-still; and though the plan was
in the end frustrated by the establishment of new rules of procedure, Parnell had at least forced the Irish question into a
position of prominence that it would hardly have attained under
Butt's milder guidance.

Butt died, broken-hearted, in 1879, and though Parnell did not
at once succeed to formal leadership, he was easily the most
important of the Irish members and soon became the most
powerful political force in Ireland. The parliamentary party
increased in numbers and prestige; but Parnell's strength did not
lie in that alone, for he had come to an agreement with the leaders
of the revolutionary movement and he had established a close
alliance with the recently formed Land League, a line of policy
usually spoken of as the 'new departure'. The accounts of
Parnell's relations with the revolutionaries are conflicting, but
the general result is clear enough. The American fenian leaders
were convinced by the effectiveness of parliamentary obstruction
that it was worth while to give the constitutional home rule
movement a chance, though they did not, of course, abandon their
own belief in force. The American support, both moral and
financial, which Parnell thus received was of enormous value to
him during the succeeding years. The third party in the alliance,
the Land League, was founded in 1879 by Michael Davitt to
protect the tenantry against rack-renting and eviction. Davitt
remained the active organiser of the League's work, but Parnell
became its president, and so the struggle for home rule and the
'land war' went forward side by side. The rapid growth and great
influence of the Land League were due in large measure to the
agricultural depression of the later 1870s, which affected the
whole British Isles. In Great Britain the decline in agriculture was
balanced by a steady rise in industrial production, but in Ireland,
except for the north-east, there was no such compensation. The
number of evictions rose sharply and the transformation of tillage
into pasture went on more rapidly than ever. The Land League
flourished in such conditions, and the enthusiasm that it aroused
greatly strengthened the home rule cause, for the two stood side
by side in opposition to the power of the landlords. Almost for

the first time, the bulk of the people were offered a political
programme of which they could see the immediate relevance to
their own condition.

For the next ten years Parnell had a difficult path to follow.
He had, in general, the greatest contempt for what the English
might think of him, but if home rule was to be achieved by
parliamentary methods he would need the help of a large section
of the British electorate, and that help would be withheld unless
he could convince them that he was neither encouraging violence
nor condoning crime. But at the same time he had to retain the
confidence of the revolutionary republicans and of the extremists
of the Land League, ever ready to resent any appearance of
truckling to the oppressor. His success was by no means complete,
but he kept the way open for an alliance with one of the British
parties while maintaining a fair degree of harmony among the
various sections of his supporters. Nationalist Ireland certainly
showed full confidence in him, and after the reform act of 1884,
which extended household franchise to Ireland and more than
tripled the electorate, the home rule party rose to eighty-six,
including seventeen out of the thirty-three Ulster members.
This election of 1885 marked the height of Parnell's power. He
held the balance between the two British parties, for though the
Liberals had a majority over the Conservatives they could not
hold office if the Irish opposed them. In these circumstances
Gladstone suddenly announced his conversion to a policy of self-
government for Ireland, and though there were immediate signs
of uneasiness among his colleagues and supporters, home rule
seemed within sight. That prospect was soon shattered. In June
1886 a home rule bill was defeated by a split in the Liberal ranks,
and the general election which followed left Gladstone in a
hopeless minority. The nationalists maintained their numerical
strength, but their freedom of action was gone, for having
thrown in their lot with the Liberals they could not hope to
succeed save in alliance with them. The extent to which this
alliance tied the nationalist party appears very clearly in the
events of 1890. Parnell's long-standing liaison with Mrs O'Shea,
the wife of one of his supporters, became public through action
in the divorce courts. His party at once affirmed its continued
loyalty, but the majority deserted him when it became known that
Gladstone and the English Liberals thought he ought to resign.
The action of the majority was strongly supported by the Roman

catholic bishops, always uneasy at protestant leadership, but it was originally dictated by English opinion. Parnell, with the help of a faithful remnant, maintained the struggle for power, and the schism in the party long survived his death in 1891. With the Liberals and the Irish nationalists weakened by internal disputes the Conservatives were able to remain almost continuously in office from 1886 to 1905. There was a brief Liberal interval from 1892 to 1895 during which Gladstone introduced a second home rule bill. It passed the commons but was rejected by the lords, who probably, on this occasion, represented pretty accurately British public opinion on the subject. When the Liberals returned to power in 1906 home rule was part of their programme; but they had at first an independent majority, and it was not until the election of January 1910 gave the Irish control of the house of commons that home rule became one of the vital issues of the day.

The history of the home rule controversy suggests two closely related questions: Why were the Irish nationalists ready to accept, and why were the English so reluctant to concede, such a strictly limited measure of autonomy? In all the home rule bills the supremacy of the imperial parliament was carefully preserved, and the powers conferred upon the Irish parliament were little more than those of an extended local government. This fell far short of the repeal of the union demanded by O'Connell and meant little or nothing to the revolutionaries who were struggling for complete separation. But most home-rulers took a common-sense view of the situation. They were prepared to accept what they could get and hope for more in the future; home rule was only a first step. 'No man', said Parnell, 'has a right to fix the boundary of the march of a nation.' It was partly by emphasising this aspect of his policy that Parnell sought to quiet the suspicions of his revolutionary allies. But many of them remained uneasy and the republican tradition survived. After his death, when the prestige of the parliamentary party declined, the movement for a violent overthrow of British rule and the establishment of a completely independent Ireland gradually gathered strength. The home rule party's relations with the Land League were simpler, for the party was always prepared to fight the cause of the tenants in parliament and in the country, and its success in this struggle did a good deal to justify it in Irish public opinion.

Gladstone's second land act (1881) went far towards satisfying
the claims of the tenants; and the policy of land-purchase,
initiated by Gladstone, was continued and extended by the
Conservatives, until Ireland was turned into a country of peasant
proprietors. The Conservative party, during its long ascendancy,
tried to combine strong government with a policy of 'killing
home rule by kindness', and the constant pressure of the
nationalists at Westminster helped to mould the social legislation
of the period in the interests of their constituents. The principles
of *laissez-faire* were now abandoned. Government support
was given to rural industries, to co-operative societies and for the
encouragement of fisheries. It cannot be said that the country
became prosperous, and, always with the exception of the north,
lack of capital remained the basic economic evil. But the most
obvious grievances of the tenant farmers were settled, and much
of the credit naturally went to the home rule party, which had
acted as their champion.

The English opposition to home rule is at first sight rather
paradoxical. Throughout the nineteenth century Englishmen
were always ready to encourage and support demands for self-
government put forward by Greeks, Serbs, Italians, Magyars,
Poles; and they considered it quite reasonable that British
colonists in Australia, South Africa and Canada should manage
their own affairs. Yet hostility to Ireland persisted; and this
hostility was particularly English: the government which passed
the home rule bill in 1912 depended for its majority on the votes
of Irish, Scottish and Welsh members. To some extent the English
attitude was dictated by obviously selfish motives: Ireland was
valuable both as a market and as a source of food supply and
her position made her of vital strategic importance to Britain.
The various home rule bills contained safeguards on these heads,
which might have satisfied legitimate anxiety; but English public
opinion was opposed to the essential principle of any sort of
self-government for Ireland, no matter how hedged about with
conditions, and no matter how costly and inconvenient the task
of keeping an unwilling partner within the union. And this
opposition was maintained with a vigour, at times with an un-
reasoning ferocity, which formed a strange contrast to the
usually calm course of English politics. English nationalism had
been stirred into action, and though it might sometimes clothe

itself in argument and parade as a reasoned policy, it was at bottom an irrational determination to maintain the integrity of what it regarded as the national territory and to impose its will upon every recalcitrant group within its borders.

This selfish English nationalism took some credit to itself for defending the interests of the unionist minority in Ireland, and particularly for supporting the claims of Ulster. But the Conservative party, which represented the nationalist spirit at its least scrupulous, regarded Irish unionism merely as an instrument of policy. Lord Randolph Churchill led the way. In the struggle over the first home rule bill he decided that 'the Orange card' was 'the one to play', and deliberately advised violent resistance if the bill should pass. 'Ulster will fight; Ulster will be right' was the watchword he left behind on his visit to Belfast in 1886. Ulster protestants took the advice more seriously, perhaps, than it was intended; but the general effect of Conservative policy, both then and later, was to encourage sectarian strife, to strengthen the separatist tendency in the north, and to make any unified settlement of the Irish problem almost impossible. Such a settlement would in any case have been difficult enough. Almost from the time at which repeal first became a serious policy the great majority of Ulster protestants had strongly denounced it, and they were just as much opposed to the more moderate proposals for limited self-government. Their traditional fear of the Roman catholic church, inflamed by O'Connell's clericalism, had not been appeased by the fact that Butt and Parnell were protestants and had some few protestant supporters. The composition, organisation and policy of the home rule party went far to justify the protestant assertion that 'home rule is Rome rule'. It was mainly on these grounds that almost all Irish protestants were unionists, but those of the north had another, and perhaps more cogent, argument, based on the economic position. Ireland since the union had not developed as an economic unit but as a complement to Great Britain, so that any weakening of the link would place some strain upon the poorer country. So far as the agricultural areas were concerned the balance could be fairly easily, and even profitably, adjusted; but the industries of the north would be ruined by separation. They did not exist to supply Irish needs, but formed part of the general British system, depending on Britain not only for markets but for essential supplies. The Ulster business man, apart altogether from any

question of security for religion, regarded home rule as a threat
to his prosperity. During the struggle over the bill of 1912 a
unionist post-card, labelled 'Belfast under home rule', showed one
of the principal streets overgrown with grass and a notice 'To let'
stuck in front of the City Hall.

The three-cornered conflict between Britain, Ulster and
nationalist Ireland reached its climax in the years immediately
preceding the first world war. The house of commons passed a
home rule bill in 1912; under the terms of the Parliament Act
of the previous year the lords could not delay it beyond 1914,
and the nationalists seemed certain of success. The opposition,
however, simply intensified the struggle. Their strong point was
clearly in Ulster, but while unionists in general wished to use
the Ulster question to defeat home rule altogether the Ulster
unionists themselves, though ready to help in this, were above
all determined to protect their own interests. Their leader, Sir
Edward Carson, a Dublin-born barrister and former attorney-
general, was mainly concerned to save all Ireland for the union,
and the true spirit of Ulster protestantism was more fully expressed
by his chief lieutenant, James Craig, afterwards Lord Craigavon
and first prime minister of Northern Ireland. Under their
direction a provisional Ulster government was set up, 'to come
into operation on the day of the passing of any home rule bill',
and a volunteer army was enrolled, drilled and armed with
German rifles. The Ulster unionists had the great advantage of
being in irresponsible opposition, and the English Conservatives,
from Bonar Law downwards, gave them open encouragement to
defy the authority of parliament by every and any means. The
nationalists, tied to a nervous government, were almost helpless,
for though they could turn the Liberals out, that would bring
home rule no nearer. John Redmond, the nationalist leader,
demanded in vain that the law should be enforced. The cabinet,
faced with a problem to which the rules of parliamentary procedure offered no solution, was inclined to wait on events, and
when it did come to the point of action found to its dismay that
the army was no longer to be relied upon. Nationalist opinion
naturally became suspicious of the government's intentions and
impatient of the policy followed by Redmond and his party.
Ulster had set a better example, and there soon came into
existence another volunteer force, this time of nationalists. The

bulk of them, it is true, accepted the leadership of Redmond; but a vigorous and influential section remained distrustful of constitutional methods. Later they separated from the main body, and in the 1916 insurrection they co-operated with the more radical 'Citizen Army', which had been founded by the Dublin labour leader, James Connolly, during a wave of strikes in 1913. But the civil war towards which Ireland seemed to be moving in the summer of 1914 was averted, temporarily, by the outbreak of a greater war in Europe. Redmond and Carson agreed to call a truce and support the government, the home rule bill was suspended for the duration of the war, and superficial harmony was established. But, in fact, Redmond no longer spoke for the most active and influential section of the nationalist movement; the events of the next few years were to destroy his leadership altogether and with it the policy of home rule which he had brought so near success.

4. THE END OF THE UNION

If the Ulster question had been peacefully settled, and if the home rule act of 1914 had come into force at once, the constitutional union between Great Britain and Ireland would have received a new lease of life, for the act was no more than a measure of devolution and left the parliament at Westminster, in which Ireland was still to be represented, with undiminished supremacy. But it is not likely that this system would have finally satisfied Irish aspirations. Already by 1914 there were forces at work which, even under home rule, would have led to a strong, and probably irresistible, movement for virtual separation. The most important of these forces were the Gaelic League, the republican tradition of violent revolution, the labour movement and Sinn Fein. The first was not avowedly political at all. It was founded in 1892 by a protestant scholar, Douglas Hyde, with the object of reviving interest in Gaelic literature, promoting Gaelic games, and, eventually, making Irish the national language. But in Ireland, as elsewhere, such a programme was really part of a reviving nationalism. All that marked Ireland off as different from England strengthened the claim that she should be treated as a distinct nation, and even those who never themselves carried the argument to that point encouraged others who did. Pearse, who was one of the men chiefly responsible for the insurrection of 1916, once said that the Gaelic League was 'the most revolutionary force that has ever come into Irish history'. He was exaggerating, but it is probably true that a majority of the leaders, and even of the rank and file, in the struggle that led up to the establishment of the Irish Free State had come under its influence.

The political importance of the Gaelic League was implicit in all that it did, and the kind of outlook that it fostered was alien to the spirit of the official nationalist party. But this did not force itself upon the notice of the party leaders, who were mainly concerned to guard against any return to revolutionary methods. Superficially, all was well; for though the Irish Republican Brotherhood had been revived, the demand for a completely independent republic had not, by 1914, expressed itself in election returns, and it had little support in the country as a whole. But the notion of an appeal to force was stimulated by the resistance of the Ulster unionists. This was looked upon with admiration as a courageous refusal by Irishmen to be bound by the laws of an English parliament, and some of the more enthusiastic republicans even dreamed of an alliance with Carson against home rule, which they detested as much as he did, though on very different grounds. Admiration led naturally to imitation, and the republicans were among the most ardent of those who helped to form the Irish volunteers. For the time being, however, they were too weak to act on their own, and had to stand aside and allow Redmond to assume control of the volunteer committee. But that control was always resented by a strong minority, and in fact the whole nature and purpose of the volunteers was incompatible with the conception of home rule. Even under Redmond's unadventurous guidance they bore witness to a nationalism more enthusiastic and intransigent than his own.

Outside the narrow ranks of the Irish Republican Brotherhood, an oath-bound secret society condemned by the Roman catholic church, republicanism was rather a sentiment, an attitude of mind, than an organised party. The most obviously active revolutionary force in Ireland in the years just before 1914 was the labour movement directed by James Connolly. The movement was essentially socialist in background and aims—its official organ was the *Workers' Republic*—but Connolly was strongly impressed by the need for the people of Ireland to control the resources of their own country before they could hope to build a socialist state, and he was prepared to fight for that independence as a necessary first step. Connolly's great importance was that he brought the urban workers over to the republican side. Since the settlement of the land problem, the driving force supplied by the grievances of the tenantry had almost disappeared and the social discontent of the towns helped to provide a substitute. It is significant that whereas the insurrections of 1798 and 1848 were rural, the only important fighting in 1916 was in Dublin. In Ireland, however, the influence of the countryside has always reasserted itself, and the workers' republic that Connolly died to establish is, to all appearance, further off now than it was then.

Connolly's effort to link the cause of Ireland with the cause of labour was not popular in his own day, and was particularly opposed by Sinn Fein.[1] This party, formally established in 1905, had grown up round a paper, *The United Irishmen*, founded some years earlier by Arthur Griffith. Griffith's object was to re-establish the constitution of 1782. He rejected violent revolution as impracticable in the circumstances of Ireland, and he condemned the constitutional methods of the parliamentary party as useless. Instead, he advocated the abstention of the Irish members from Westminster and the formation of a voluntary 'parliament' and system of arbitration courts to rule the country and maintain order by moral force. Both in the end at which he aimed and in the methods which he proposed to use Griffith was mainly inspired by the policy of the Hungarian deputies in the 1860s, and his programme was commonly spoken of as the 'Hungarian policy'. Sinn Fein was concerned with economics as well as with politics. Griffith believed that Ireland could be made self-supporting and that with proper encouragement and protection she could become an industrial as well as an agricultural country. But, though he rejected the doctrine of free trade, his economic outlook was in other respects typically nineteenth century; in particular, he had a strong respect for capital and condemned the labour movement and the strikes of 1913. In later years Sinn Fein policy was modified in many respects. The use of force was accepted, the 'Irish republic' replaced the 'constitution of 1782', and the need for reforming social conditions was recognised. The fact that Connolly at the same time was moving towards a more strongly nationalist position made possible the co-operation of the Sinn Fein and labour forces in 1916.

1. The name 'Sinn Fein' ('we ourselves') was meant to indicate the policy of political and economic self-reliance advocated by the party.

The year 1916 is the turning-point in the last phase of the legislative union. The outbreak of war with Germany had brought a temporary easing of the Irish situation. There was, both north and south, genuine sympathy for the allied cause. Industry and agriculture prospered. The country as a whole was prepared to wait for 'the end of the war'—the Ulster unionists with undiminished determination to resist home rule, the parliamentary nationalists with an ill-founded confidence in the willingness and ability of the British government to satisfy their claims. The small minority of separatists—republicans, socialists, Sinn Feiners—had little immediate influence on public opinion; but they drew steadily closer together and became more and more convinced that the war offered an opportunity for successful rebellion. Part of their plan was to secure German help, and negotiations were carried out by Sir Roger Casement, a former British colonial civil servant. But it was clear that so long as Britain had command of the sea German help, if it came at all, would be on a small scale; in the end, a project for landing arms on the coast of Kerry failed completely. Despite this, the republican leaders pressed on with their plans. They knew that they had little or no hope of immediate military success; their aim was to arouse the conscience of the people. 'There has been nothing more terrible in Irish history', wrote Pearse, 'than the failure of the last generation.' He and his colleagues believed intensely that only a sacrifice of blood could redeem that failure. The insurrection of 1916 was not the result of intolerable oppression, nor did it begin with any reasonable prospect of success; but though the fighting was over in a week the most astute political calculation could hardly have found a more effective way of arousing and uniting national sentiment.

For a very brief period it seemed as if the insurrection had failed in its purpose, for the immediate reaction of Irish nationalist opinion was to condemn it as criminal folly. But the government's treatment of the affair, however natural in the circumstances, produced an immediate revulsion of feeling. Fifteen of the insurgents were tried by court martial and shot. Had this been done immediately after the insurrection Irish opinion would probably have accepted it as a necessary protective measure by a government already fighting for its life. But the executions were dragged out over a period of several days, even after it seemed clear that the danger was over; the initiative in

propaganda was left to the handful of republican sympathisers,
who were encouraged and helped by the strongly anti-British
attitude of the American press, and within a short time many
of those who had condemned the rising were exalting its leaders
as martyrs. The whole political atmosphere had suddenly changed.
The uneasy suspicion with which many people had long regarded
the policy of home rule turned into a burning contempt—
republicanism had become the dominant political creed.

The insurrection had been mainly the work of the Irish
Republican Brotherhood and the Citizen Army, but it was Sinn
Fein which provided the machinery to take advantage of the
rising tide of republicanism. In one by-election after another
Sinn Fein candidates were returned, and the home rule party
hastened its own overthrow by inflaming anti-British feeling and
by an abortive experiment with the policy of abstention from
attendance at parliament, which amounted almost to a confession
of failure. The government's proposal to extend conscription to
Ireland in 1918, though it brought about a temporary alliance
of Nationalists and Sinn Feiners, really worked in favour of the
latter. The anti-conscription movement, in which Roman catholic
Ireland was practically unanimous, went far to destroy the last
shreds of confidence in Britain, and so weakened still further the
prestige of the parliamentary party. The effect of all this became
clear in the general election of 1918. Of the hundred and five
Irish seats Sinn Fein won seventy-three, the unionists twenty-six
(all but three of them in Ulster), the home-rulers only six. It was
a verdict against home rule rather than in favour of a republic
and the result was undoubtedly influenced by wide-spread
intimidation; but it marked the end of the old parliamentary
nationalism and it gave Sinn Fein a claim to represent the will of
the country. Before this disaster to his life's work Redmond had
died, having added another name to the list of Ireland's rejected
leaders.

Sinn Fein had abandoned both its objection to the use of force
and its limited constitutional programme, and was now prepared
to fight, if necessary, for an independent Irish republic. But it
still retained a part of its 'Hungarian policy'. After the election
the Sinn Fein members refused to go to Westminster; instead,
they met together, assumed the title 'Dail Eireann' ('Assembly of
Ireland') and declared their allegiance to the republic proclaimed

F

by the insurgents in 1916. Eamon de Valera, the most important of the surviving 1916 leaders, was elected president, and a ministry was appointed which claimed to be the legitimate government of Ireland. The republicans placed a good deal of faith in the force of foreign opinion, especially in America, and one of their first acts was to elect delegates to the peace conference at Paris. But neither Wilson nor Clemenceau wished to embarrass the British government, and the delegates were refused recognition. The republicans were more successful at home than abroad. They dominated a majority of the various bodies which controlled local government, and in many areas voluntary arbitration courts, recognising the authority of the Dail, exercised a far more effective jurisdiction than the courts of the crown. But such a situation could not last long without open and forcible defiance of British authority, and from the beginning of 1919 onwards armed clashes between the crown forces and the republicans became more frequent and more serious, until in July 1921 a truce was arranged as a preliminary to a permanent settlement.

Historians and politicians often refer to the events of these years as the 'Anglo-Irish war'. Ordinary people are satisfied to speak more simply, and perhaps more accurately, of the 'troubles'. The struggle was not so much between two governments or two peoples as between two largely irresponsible armed forces. The British government found the greatest difficulty in exercising effective control over the auxiliary police and the 'Black-and-Tans'[1] on whom the bulk of the fighting fell, and the Dail had little choice but to leave the 'Irish Republican Army' to carry out operations in its own way and on its own responsibility. It was not until April 1921, when the struggle was nearly over, that de Valera, in the name of the Dail, took explicit responsibility for the war policy of the republican army. It was this lack of unified control on the Irish side that led to the outbreak of civil war when the British forces were withdrawn. A later generation, familiar with underground resistance movements, can appreciate the difficulties of both sides more fully than contemporaries could. The British government had the moral duty of keeping order, protecting property and maintaining some semblance of civil administration in the face of the open or concealed opposition of the great

1. A special force enlisted from among British ex-servicemen; so called from their mixed military and police uniform.

majority of the population. If they had been ready to regard
Ireland as hostile territory they could easily have crushed
resistance and established effective military rule; but to have
done so would have been to destroy their moral right to be in the
country at all. On the republican side there were all the difficulties
arising from shortage of money, arms and ammunition; and all
the problems facing a government carried on in secret. It has
been calculated that the republican army never had more than
three thousand men in action at once, and they were quite
incapable of undertaking regular military operations, for which,
indeed, there was little opportunity in a war without a frontier.
Their methods were ambushes, assassinations and raids. They
wore no uniform and could easily emerge from and disappear
into the civilian population. The crown forces, driven almost to
distraction by the attacks of a ruthless and elusive enemy, adopted
a policy of reprisals, sometimes with, sometimes without, the
approval of the authorities. It was a war in which victory was
impossible. The British might have restored order, but they
could not have established the state of mutual confidence necessary for democratic government. The republicans could and did
make normal administration impossible, but they could never, in
their own strength, have driven the British out. The main factor
in bringing the war to an end was not the force of arms, but the
force of British public opinion. What the war did accomplish
was the preparation of both sides for a compromise.

The necessity for compromise, implicit from the beginning
in this as in most other struggles, was emphasised by the position
of Ulster. Unionism as a serious political force had disappeared
from the rest of Ireland, but in Ulster it was stronger than ever,
and the claims and methods of the republican forces went far
towards making a united Ireland impossible. The British government, anxious for some sort of settlement as speedily as possible,
had passed, in 1920, the Government of Ireland Act, which made
provision for two Irish parliaments, one in the north and the
other in the south. The northern parliament, with its seat at
Belfast, was to legislate for the six counties of Antrim, Armagh,
Down, Fermanagh, Londonderry and Tyrone, which together
had a protestant majority, though with a strong and locally-
dominant Roman catholic minority. A parliament at Dublin
was to legislate for the rest of the country, and a 'Council of

Ireland' was to consider matters of common interest. The powers
of the two parliaments were to be similar to those conferred by
the home rule act of 1914 and Irish representation at Westminster
was to continue. As a result of this act the new state of Northern
Ireland came into existence in 1921.

This safeguarding of the Ulster unionists was the main result of
the act; for it had no chance of acceptance in the south, where
the struggle continued as before. The republicans made great
efforts to prevent the northern government from functioning.
Even before that government had come into existence Belfast and
some other areas in Ulster had been seriously disturbed by
sectarian riots, in which the Roman catholics, as the weaker
party, had suffered heavily. But now a concerted effort, organised
by I.R.A. headquarters, was made to disrupt civil administration
altogether, and the initial refusal of the Roman catholic population to co-operate in working the constitution of the new state
laid them open to suspicion of complicity in the republican
campaign. The Northern Ireland government, with British
military resources to back it up, was able to restore order and
establish its authority, but the long and bitter struggle left an
enduring mark on the character of the régime.

The British government, having salved its conscience with
regard to Ulster, was anxious for a compromise with the republicans. Foreign opinion, especially in the United States, was
increasingly hostile, and the task of convincing a sceptical world
of the justice of Britain's claims in Ireland was becoming almost
mpossible. At home, there was public uneasiness about the
object and the methods of a war which seemed to be fought
against the very principle of self-determination. The stories
published in the newspapers might be exaggerated, partial and
ill-informed, but the conscience of the country was stirred and
refused to be satisfied with the answer that the atrocities of the
republicans exceeded those of the Black-and-Tans. The republicans, for their part, were ready to welcome a respite. Their ranks
were depleted by casualties and captures, they were finding it
increasingly difficult to obtain arms and ammunition, and the
country was getting tired of the fighting. When Lloyd George's
invitation to negotiate came, rather suddenly, in June 1921, they
were almost at the end of their resources. Early next month a
truce was arranged, and the work of finding a compromise
began.

The history of the negotiations, which extended over several months, is a confused one and, on the Irish side, a subject of bitter dispute. But from the beginning the essence of the position was clear to all men of common sense: both sides must make substantial concessions, and the only alternative to a settlement was a renewal of war. Lloyd George had explicitly stated that Ireland could not be allowed to sever herself completely from the British Empire and that Ulster must not be coerced. These conditions being accepted, every other subject was open for discussion. The leaders of the Irish delegation, Arthur Griffith and Michael Collins, were essentially practical men. Griffith had always disliked the use of force and was mainly interested in economic and administrative problems. He saw in Lloyd George's offer of dominion status an approach to his own 'Hungarian policy', and he was at least partly responsible for inducing his colleagues to accept it. Collins had played a leading part in the struggle of the previous two years and had won a great reputation for courage and skill; he knew how precarious the position of the republican forces was and how difficult it would be to continue if the British government chose to exert its full strength. In these circumstances a treaty[1] was signed on 6 December 1921. Ireland was to become a self-governing dominion of the British Commonwealth, under the style of the 'Irish Free State', and was specifically guaranteed the same degree of constitutional independence as the dominion of Canada. In practice, this did not fall far short of a republican settlement; but there were three limitations which the Irish delegates had accepted very reluctantly: members of parliament were to take an oath of allegiance to the crown, in virtue of Ireland's membership of the British Commonwealth; Northern Ireland was to be left free to stay out of the new dominion and continue its existing constitutional position within the United Kingdom; the British government retained peace-time naval establishments in certain Irish ports. It was these conditions, and the first in particular, which aroused the strongest opposition when the terms came to be debated in the Dail. De Valera himself, who had taken no direct part in the later stages of the negotiations, led the attack and supported it with all the glamour of his reputation and all the

1. On the British side the official term is 'articles of agreement', but 'treaty' is in much more common use, and on the Irish side has always been insisted upon, as implying the sovereign status of the republican government.

emotional force of an appeal to the inviolable rights of the republic. Griffith, the mainstay of the defence, was a less romantic figure. He ignored juridical subtleties and emotional appeal, and confined himself to the common-sense line of argument that he and his colleagues had been sent to London 'not as republican doctrinaires, but looking for the substance of freedom and independence'; that the treaty, in spite of many defects, did give that substance, and that it need not be regarded as a final settlement. After long and bitter debates, which lasted until 7 January 1922, the treaty was accepted by the Dail, and a week later a provisional government under Michael Collins was set up to take over authority from the British. There were further formalities to be gone through, but the legislative union, after its hundred and twenty years of uneasy existence, had, in fact, come to an end.

To Irish nationalists the legislative union is a period of oppression and degradation, to the Irish unionists a great experiment which went wrong; to the historian its main characteristic is that it made possible the Irish nation of today. By surrendering their political independence in 1800 the protestant landlords gained a temporary security for their privileges but lost the power to defend them for the future, and the gradual destruction of those privileges by successive British governments left the way open for the rise of the Roman catholic peasantry and middle class to a dominant position. In 1800, the alternative to union seemed to be either the survival of an intransigent protestant ascendancy or its replacement by a revolutionary Ireland, governed according to the principles of French enlightenment. It was the peace imposed by Britain that made possible the emergence of a third force, the Roman catholic nation, which was sustained by protestant leadership and revolutionary fervour, but was strong enough to keep its own character against both. 'When I was a boy', said one of the Beresfords in the mid-nineteenth century, ' "the Irish people" meant the protestants, now it means the Roman catholics.' The social and political transformation which this implies was, for good or ill, the great legacy of the union to Ireland.

6

IRELAND SINCE THE TREATY

The legislative union had been established in the middle of a desperate war, and the main motive on the British side had been military security. Its dissolution came after an even greater war had been brought to a victorious conclusion and at a time when peace and self-confidence made British public opinion particularly disposed towards a generous settlement. There was, therefore, in 1921 and 1922 a serious desire to meet the needs and claims of Ireland, a desire that had been almost completely lacking in 1800. Yet in spite of this contrast both the union and its dissolution suffered from the same defect, in that both failed to solve the two radical problems that stood in the way of a permanent and peaceful settlement of Irish affairs: the internal problem of relations between Roman catholic and protestant, and the external problem of relations between Ireland and Great Britain. The Government of Ireland Act and the treaty changed the form but not the substance of these problems. The old conflict of interests between the protestant ascendancy and the Roman catholic masses had gone, but it was replaced by the political division between Northern Ireland, with its predominantly protestant population, and the rest of the country; and within Northern Ireland mutal fears and suspicions kept sectarian conflict alive. This situation in turn left an element of uneasiness in Anglo-Irish relations. The two countries were, however, bound closely together by a common economic interest; and this link, though resented by some Irishmen as essentially a continuation of British imperialism, was so strong that no Dublin government could afford permanently to ignore it. The failure of the treaty settlement to bring complete harmony to Anglo-Irish relations was in some measure qualified by the operation of economic forces.

The signing of the treaty did not put an immediate end to the fighting in Ireland. In the north, the I.R.A. campaign against the new régime continued, even after Collins had agreed, in March 1922, to call off his forces. In the rest of the country, disagreement over the terms of the treaty led, within a few months, to the outbreak of a civil war. The first reaction to the treaty had, indeed, been one of relief; but doctrinaire republicanism was strong both in the I.R.A. and among the political leaders. Though the Dail approved the treaty, after a long and acrimonious debate, and though a general election in June 1922 returned a pro-treaty majority, the republican die-hards refused to accept this verdict. On the political side, their opposition was organised by de Valera; on the military side, they had the support of a large section of the I.R.A.—it was, indeed, the division in the army rather than among the politicians or in the country at large that led directly to civil war. The new Free State government, under Arthur Griffith and Michael Collins, was at first reluctant to force the issue; but the aggressive action of their opponents left them no alternative, and by the end of June open hostilities had broken out.

The republicans now used against the Free State all the methods which in previous years had been used against the British. They could no longer, however, count on the same public support, and their wholesale destruction of property and frequent bank-robberies, together with the suspicion that they favoured a communist land-policy, turned a population heartily sick of rule by revolver more and more against them. Besides this, the new government showed energy, determination and courage, and, above all, a ruthlessness that the British had never dared to display.[1] They executed scores of prisoners and left hunger-strikers to starve if they chose. These measures had their effect, and in May 1923 de Valera announced the end of resistance. But it was beyond his power to control the forces that years of irregular warfare had unloosed, and the threat of violence remained part of the background of Irish political life.

1. Miss Macardle, in her republican apologia, lists forty republicans executed by the British between 1916 and 1921, and seventy-seven executed by the Free State government in 1922 and 1923. (D. Macardle, *The Irish republic* (London, 1927), pp. 1023–5).

The civil war had had the effect of easing republican pressure on the north, and there also the effective authority of government had been established by 1923. The struggle in the north had, inevitably, followed sectarian lines. To the protestants, the separate status of the six-county area was the only guarantee against domination by a Dublin parliament. To the Roman catholics, it meant condemnation to the position of a permanent minority. Naturally enough, many of them gave active support to the republican attack; and throughout the province it was in the predominantly Roman catholic areas that the republicans had their strongholds. Ulster protestants had long believed that Roman catholics were essentially 'disloyal'; they regarded the events of the early 1920s as confirmation of this belief; and when peace was at length restored the prospects of reconciliation between the two sections of the population seemed further off than ever. The old equations of 'protestant' with 'unionist' and of 'Roman catholic' with 'nationalist' still stood; and in the confined area of Northern Ireland these equations were bound to have a stultifying effect on political life.

Decade after decade the leaders, on both sides, stuck to their traditional attitudes. The main object of the unionists was to make sure that every protestant voter supported the unionist party; and they hardly even thought of trying to broaden its scope by an appeal to the minority. The nationalists were no less sectarian. They based themselves exclusively on those areas that were predominantly Roman catholic, and nationalist M.P.s regarded the defence of catholic interests as their main function. So complete and so rigid was the division that there was no room for any third force. A struggling labour party, itself split over the question of partition, did succeed in returning a few members to parliament; but their presence there did not change the general character of the situation.

There was nothing new in this sectarianism, which had existed for generations. What was new, since 1920, was that the protestants now had continuous control of the organs of administration; and they used this control, together with the influence they derived from their economic superiority, to make sure that their own predominance and their majority position should continue indefinitely. A Roman catholic seeking employment, or housing, or advancement in his career, generally found himself at a heavy disadvantage in competition with protestants; and for many the only escape lay in emigration: though the birth-rate among Roman catholics was higher than among protestants, the Roman catholic proportion of the population showed little increase during the first forty years of the Northern Ireland régime. From the unionist viewpoint, this general distrust of Roman catholics was justified on the grounds of their attitude in the past and their continued support for the merging of Northern Ireland with the rest of the country under the Dublin government. But, whatever the force of this argument, there was little in the policy of the unionist party that might induce the northern nationalists to change their views and accept the existing situation as final. The peace established in the early 1920s had only strengthened and embittered the rivalry between the opposing groups. On both sides, the leaders were men whose views had been formed during the bitter years of the Home Rule controversy. The first prime minister of Northern Ireland was Sir James Craig,[1] who had been Carson's principal lieutenant; and the chief representative of the nationalist minority was Joseph Devlin, formerly a prominent member of the Home Rule party. Though they were men of long experience and basic common sense, they had little freedom of manœuvre: Craig could not escape from the position in which the unionists had entrenched themselves in the early 1920s; and Devlin was the spokesman of the catholic minority rather than the effective leader of an organised political movement.

In the south, also, the events of those years had a continuing influence, for political attitudes were long determined by the divisions established during the civil war. Thus, in both parts of the country, normal political development was hampered; and the electorate was often more easily moved by the invocation of men and movements of the past than by any consideration of the actual circumstances in which everyday life had to be lived.

This virtual stagnation of politics survived so long mainly because of the importance attached by all parties to the question of partition. It is true that this had not been a major issue in the civil war; but both sides in that struggle had believed that the question would soon settle itself. The treaty had provided for a modification of the boundary between Northern Ireland and the rest of the country; and nationalists of all shades of opinion were convinced that the result would be the speedy disappearance of Northern Ireland as a separate political unit. In fact, however,

1. Created Viscount Craigavon, 1927.

when a boundary commission was later set up, it accomplished nothing, and in 1925 the existing boundary was accepted as definitive by the governments of the United Kingdom, Northern Ireland and the Irish Free State. But, despite this, successive Dublin governments continued to demand the ending of partition and the inclusion of the six-county area under their jurisdiction. While this was the prevailing attitude in Dublin the northern unionist was not likely to feel secure, nor was the northern nationalist likely to give up hope; and neither was likely to accept the necessity for compromise.

Though the question of partition was thus a central one, it would be a mistake to suppose that partition itself was the cause of the unhealthy state of Irish politics. Partition was not a cause, but a symptom. It had been imposed by a British government as a means of solving an age-old problem; and, though it had failed in its purpose, the problem would not now be solved, even if its form would be changed, by a mere reversal of policy. The forced inclusion of the northern protestants in an all-Ireland state could lead only to a civil war, the ferocity and destructiveness of which it is easy to imagine, but to the duration of which no likely limit could be foreseen. Some observers were impressed by the fact that the protestant minority in the south had accepted the new régime there, and had been well treated by the government. But the southern protestants were too small a body to be politically significant; and, in any case, their numbers had declined sharply and continuously since the establishment of the Free State, and they seemed doomed to disappear almost completely within a few generations. The strongly-knit and growing protestant population in the north was in a very different position.

The partition question, however stultifying its influence, was often useful to politicians on both sides of the border, and they never allowed the electorate to forget it for long. But, at the same time, the routine business of government had to go on; and during the half-century that followed the treaty Ireland had to be guided through great social and economic changes. For Northern Ireland, as an integral part of the United Kingdom, all major decisions were taken at Westminster; and the Northern Ireland government could have only a marginal influence on the shaping of the total economy. Within fairly narrow limits, however, it could and did take the initiative: its agricultural policy produced an enormous improvement in the standard of farming; and its constant efforts to introduce new industries helped to reduce the traditional dependence on textiles, engineering and shipbuilding, all of which were tending to decline. In social legislation it had greater freedom of action; but the unionists adopted a 'step by step' principle, which meant that Northern Ireland followed British example fairly closely. There were some local variations, due partly to the special circumstances of the province and partly to the very conservative outlook of the unionist leadership; but, broadly speaking, economic and social development in the north followed the British model. There was, in fact, little opportunity, even if there had been the desire, to re-shape society on new and independent lines. In the south, it was very different. Though the conflict over the terms of the treaty remained, even after 1923, as the major political issue, the life of the country was far more profoundly affected by economic and social changes on which all parties were in broad agreement.

The Free State had emerged from the civil war under new leadership: Griffith died in 1922 and Collins was killed in an ambush in the same year. The new head of the government was W. T. Cosgrave, a quietly-efficient administrator. He was without the vigour and force of character of Collins, who had been his predecessor, or of de Valera, who was to follow him; but he retained office for ten troublesome years and he gave the new state a respectable stability that it might not have acquired under more adventurous guidance. The outstanding member of his cabinet was Kevin O'Higgins, minister for justice, whose stern measures of repression helped to stamp out political crime, though they also led to his own assassination in 1927. But the same year saw a long step towards the establishment of normal political conditions. De Valera and his followers, though numerically the strongest of the opposition parties, had hitherto been excluded from the Dail by their refusal to take the oath of allegiance prescribed in the treaty; now they changed their attitude, in fact if not in theory, and, after a general election in 1927, they took their seats.[1] Their advent weakened the position of the Cosgrave government, which now had to rely on the support of other parties; but it had already laid down clearly the lines along which future policy was to develop.

1. Not all the anti-treaty forces accepted de Valera's policy of entering the Dail. Those who did so were organised in a new political party under the title Fianna Fail. The Cosgrave party was known as Cumann na nGaedheal, later changed to Fine Gael.

In this policy three principal objects can be distinguished: first, to weaken the constitutional connection with Britain and to emphasise the sovereign independence of the state; secondly, to encourage manufacturing industry, and thus reduce dependence upon imports from Britain; thirdly, to promote the 'Gaelicisation' of Irish society. In pursuing the first of these objects the Cosgrave government confined itself within the limits imposed by the treaty. Thus, for example, it took an important share in the discussions leading up to the Statute of Westminster, by which the sovereign status of the dominions was formally recognised; but it refused to abolish the oath of allegiance. At the same time, however, it was careful to insist that its relations with the crown should be direct and formal, and in no way controlled or supervised by the British government. But all this was, in reality, little more than a matter of prestige. The policies followed at home had far greater importance, both immediately and for the future.

Griffith had looked forward to political independence as a means of establishing economic independence also; and, true to his principles, the Free State government had quickly imposed a wide range of protective tariffs. As a result, some new industries were set up; and some British manufacturers, anxious to keep their place in the Irish market, established subsidiary companies in Ireland. But there was a lack of capital and experience; and, in any case, the Irish and British economies were so closely intermingled, and the predominance of Britain so strongly established, that fundamental changes in the situation were hardly possible without a much more revolutionary policy than any Irish government was likely to venture on. The efforts of the Cosgrave government and its successors were certainly not fruitless; and the economy became gradually more diversified. But the dream of an Ireland with large and expanding manufacturers and a steadily-growing population remained no more than a dream.

If the economic policy of the Free State was derived from Griffith, its culture policy was inspired by Pearse, whose ideal had been an Ireland 'not free only, but Gaelic as well'. It now became the aim of government to Gaelicise every aspect of Irish life and, more especially, to extend the use of the Irish language. It became an essential part of the curriculum in all schools subsidised by the state, and great encouragement was given to the teaching of other subjects through the medium of

Irish. A knowledge of it was required from all civil servants; and it was given official status in government documents and publications. But the policy had little obvious success: English remained the language of ordinary life everywhere except in those remote western areas which had an unbroken Gaelic-speaking tradition. Yet even the obligation to learn the language had its effect; and this was strengthened by the emphasis constantly laid on what were considered the essentially Gaelic elements in Irish history and tradition. Thus, even people who rarely spoke Irish and who, perhaps, understood it very imperfectly, nevertheless became accustomed to the idea of a Gaelic distinctiveness. This fell far short of Pearse's ideal; but it marked a real change in what one might call the cultural atmosphere.

These policies, inaugurated by the Cosgrave administration, were continued and extended by its successor. After the general election of 1932 de Valera's Fianna Fail was the largest single party, though without an absolute majority in the Dail. There was, however, sufficient support from minor groups to enable de Valera to form a government, and he entered upon a period of office that lasted continuously until 1948.

The most striking characteristic of this long period was a steady weakening of the British connection. De Valera was not restrained, as his predecessor had been, by regard for the terms of the treaty; and one of the first acts of his government was to remove the oath of allegiance from the constitution. Almost at the same time he became involved in a dispute with Britain over payments to be made by the Free State under the terms of financial agreements concluded in 1923 and 1926.[1] When these payments were withheld in 1932 the British government retaliated by imposing tariffs on Free State goods imported into the United Kingdom; and the dispute developed into an 'economic war'. The Free State government used this as an opportunity to intensify the policy of economic self-sufficiency, and also made great efforts to direct the country's overseas trade away from the United Kingdom; but, though it was fairly easy to find alternative sources of supply for goods formerly imported from Britain, it proved almost impossible to find any other market for Irish exports. Thus the policy of economic separation from Britain had no more than a partial and somewhat precarious success.

1. The most important of these payments consisted of the annuities still being collected under the terms of the various land-purchase acts.

The concomitant policy of constitutional separation achieved more permanent results. In 1936 the Free State government took advantage of the abdication of Edward VIII to pass the External Relations Act, which practically removed the crown from the constitution, except for formal diplomatic purposes. A further step was taken in the following year, with the promulgation of an entirely new constitution, which was in all essential respects republican and not monarchical, though the term 'republic' was not used and though the crown still retained the functions allotted to it by the act of 1936. Much more significant was the fact that the constitution claimed to be a constitution for the whole island: the term 'Irish Free State' was abandoned and 'Ireland' (Eire) substituted.[1] The British government rejected the idea that this claim could affect the existing constitutional position of Northern Ireland; but, in other respects, it was prepared to recognise the new constitution. Both sides were, in fact, now anxious to settle their differences; and in 1938 Chamberlain and de Valera reached a comprehensive agreement. The financial dispute was settled by a compromise; and the British government undertook to withdraw its forces from the 'treaty parts', where it had maintained establishments since 1921—a concession of which the full importance was soon to be revealed when the United Kingdom became involved in the second world war.

The neutrality of Eire during this war was a clear demonstration of the extent and reality of her separation from Britain and the rest of the Commonwealth. But neutrality was, in the circumstances, a natural policy to follow, for the reasons that had forced upon Britain a tardy decision to resist German aggression did not affect Eire with anything like the same urgency. Besides, there was still an active group of republican extremists who had never accepted de Valera's decision to adopt constitutional means; they maintained a military organisation, 'the Irish Republican Army' (I.R.A.), and they regarded England as the only enemy. Any attempt to bring Eire into the war on the allied side could have provoked such widespread and violent resistance that government might well have been paralysed. A state built upon revolutionary principles can rarely afford to run such risks, and

1. The constitution was published both in Irish and in English. In the English version the name of the state is given as 'Ireland'; but in normal English usage the Irish name 'Eire' was used to indicate the twenty-six counties.

neutrality was probably the safest policy to follow. For Britain, now that she had given up the treaty ports, this neutrality meant a dangerous weakening of her western defences; and the government in London seriously considered occupying Eire by force. Only the fact that Northern Ireland was still part of the United Kingdom made it possible to refrain from this action without fatally exposing overseas communications. It was thus the partition of Ireland that enabled the greater part of the country to escape the full rigours of war, though thousands of volunteers from Eire did, in fact, join the British forces.

Eire's neutrality provided the northern unionists with another justification of their refusal to leave the United Kingdom; but long before this the whole trend of de Valera's policy had confirmed them in their belief that they had little common ground with the bulk of their fellow-countrymen. Their economy was so closely tied to that of Great Britain that they could not afford to have tariff barriers set up; and the steady whittling away of the constitutional connection destroyed any likelihood of their being able to enter a united Ireland which would be an active and cooperative member of the British Commonwealth. But, apart altogether from this, there were elements in the policy pursued by Dublin governments since 1922 that seemed, at least to northern protestants, to indicate an intention of turning Ireland into an essentially Gaelic and catholic state. The language policy inaugurated in the 1920s was continued even more energetically, though with little more appearance of success, under de Valera. So far as religion was concerned, the government's attitude was, at first, one of formal neutrality; though the denial of the right of civil divorce, in 1925, suggested a readiness to bring the law of the state into line with Roman catholic teaching. But a new policy was made explicit in the constitution of 1937, which accorded a special status to the Roman catholic church. These policies were quite appropriate to the twenty-six county area; and here, though they aroused some criticism, they met no serious opposition. But they were put forward specifically as policies for all Ireland and for all Irishmen; and, as such, they were seen by northern unionists as a clear indication of the kind of treatment they might expect if the country were to be re-united.

When one considers the attitudes of the two Irish governments one can hardly help observing that, however much they might differ in other respects, they shared a common insensitiveness

to minority opinion. The government in Belfast administered
Northern Ireland as if the whole population should conform to
(or, at least, accept as normal) the patterns imposed by the protestant and unionist majority. The government in Dublin planned
the new and united Ireland to which it looked forward on the
implicit assumption that the northern protestants would have
to abandon their distinctive characteristics and be submerged in
a predominantly Gaelic and catholic community. Wolfe Tone
might be denounced in the north and idolised in the south;
but his principles were disregarded equally in both parts of the
country.

De Valera did not give formal expression to the spirit of his
policy by declaring a republic, perhaps because he hesitated to
break the last link, however tenuous, with the other nations of
the Commonwealth. His failure to do so increased the resentment
with which he was regarded by republican extremists, and was one
of the factors that led to his defeat in the general election of
February 1948, though this was mainly due to the natural reaction
of public opinion after sixteen years of government by one party
or, rather, by one man, for de Valera had dominated both Fianna
Fail and the country. After the election Fianna Fail, though
still the largest party in the Dail, no longer had a majority; and
the desire for a change of government was so general and so
strong that all the other parties, despite the opposing programmes
on which they had fought the election, joined in a coalition held
together by no common principle except that of keeping de
Valera out of office.

To the surprise of most, and the consternation of many, this
new government decided to take the final step in the process of
separation. In September 1948 the prime minister, J. A. Costello,
then on a visit to Ottawa, announced that legislation would
shortly be introduced to sever the last constitutional link between Eire and the Commonwealth by repealing the External
Relations Act. Before the end of the year this had been done; and
on Easter Monday 1949 the republic was formally inaugurated.
The change, which was generally recognised as one of name only,
aroused little enthusiasm in Ireland and no resentment in Britain.
The removal of the crown from the constitution made no practical
difference; and in other respects everything went on as before.
By arrangement between Dublin and London, citizens of the

republic were not to be treated as aliens in the United Kingdom, nor British citizens as aliens in the republic. Though the diplomatic representatives exchanged by the two governments now became 'ambassadors' instead of 'high commissioners', Irish affairs continued to be dealt with by the Commonwealth Relations Office, so long as it retained a separate existence. It is, perhaps, hardly surprising that the I.R.A. and its supporters refused to accept the republic of 1949 as a substitute for the republic of 1916, to which alone they professed allegiance; and the new régime, like its predecessors, had to face the recurrent threat of internal violence.

The course of events had been watched with great anxiety in the north. Though the constitutional change had been so much a matter of form, the Dublin government had used the occasion to reiterate its claim to authority over the whole island and had launched a vigorous propaganda campaign against partition, accompanied by bitter denunciations of the unionist party. The effect on Northern Ireland of this propaganda was demonstrated at a general election in February 1949, when the appearance of anti-partition candidates subsidised from the south led only to an increase in the unionist vote and a strengthening of the government's position in parliament. What the unionists really feared, however, was the effect of propaganda in Britain. Since 1945, they had had to deal, almost for the first time, with a Labour government at Westminster; and not only was Labour traditionally sympathetic to Irish nationalism, but there were many constituencies where Labour members depended heavily on the votes of Irish immigrants. In fact, however, unionist fears proved groundless; and the legislation passed by the British parliament in 1949 to regulate relations with the new republic expressly provided that no change should be made in the constitutional status of Northern Ireland without the consent of the Northern Ireland parliament.

In one respect, 1949 marked the end of a period: so far as the twenty-six-county area was concerned, the treaty of 1921 had now been reversed, the last symbol of British authority removed, and the country left completely free to go its own way. But there remained the question of partition. From the British point of view, this was a matter to be settled between north and south: if the parliament of Northern Ireland expressed a wish to enter the republic no difficulty would be made. But the government of

the republic saw the situation differently. It insisted that partition
was imposed by Britain; and refused either to recognise the
constitutional status of Northern Ireland or to admit that the
Northern Ireland parliament had any right to determine the
future of the province. This divergence of outlook had, however,
little practical effect on Anglo-Irish relations. The republic
constantly advertised its sense of grievance; but it either would
not or could not take any positive action; and the partition
question gradually acquired an air of unreality. Political leaders
in the republic continued to talk about it; but in practice they
accepted the existing situation and acted as if it were to last
indefinitely.

This acquiescent attitude was, of course, condemned by the
extremere publican groups, of which the I.R.A. was the most
important. But their own efforts met with such ill-success that
they merely served to show how the political atmosphere was
changing. During the 1950s they maintained a sporadic campaign of terrorism in the north, only to find themselves condemned
both by the leaders of the northern nationalists, to whom they
might have looked for support, and by public opinion in the
south, where the government took strong measures to suppress
their activities. It seemed, now, as if old quarrels were dying and
as if Ireland might move, even if slowly, towards some sort of
stability based upon the *status quo*.

The mere passage of time contributed to this development.
By 1960 the border had been in existence for forty years, and
the effect, on both parts of the country, of such a long period of
separation could not be unfelt. But there were other influences
also. Constitutional independence had not altered the fact that
Ireland was part of the British economic system.[1] The attempt
to break away from this in the 1930s had failed; and during the
1950s and 1960s successive governments in Dublin had shown
themselves not only ready to accept the situation but increasingly
anxious for closer integration. In 1965 when Fianna Fail was once
more in office, under de Valera's successor, Sean Lemass, a

1. In 1960 the total value of exports from the republic was *c* £152 millions.
Of this, *c* £91 millions went to Great Britain; *c* £19 millions to Northern Ireland;
c £11 millions to the U.S.A. (the republic's third best customer). The value of the
republic's imports was *c* £226 millions, of which *c* £104 millions came from Great
Britain and *c* £13 millions from Northern Ireland. (In the same year, the total
value of exports from Great Britain was *c* £3,000 millions and from Northern
Ireland *c* £335 millions.)

comprehensive commercial treaty was concluded with Britain.
This provided for a progressive reduction of tariffs on both sides,
and was meant to lead to the establishment of an Anglo-Irish
free-trade area by 1975.

The republican government's readiness to strengthen economic
links with Britain without pressing the question of partition
reflects its general attitude at this period. The claim to jurisdiction
over the six-county area was not abandoned, or even modified;
but it gradually fell into the background both with politicians
and with the public at large. This change of attitude in the south
contributed to a gradual easing, already apparent, of internal
tensions in the north. Among unionists, there was a growing
body who believed that the constitution could be maintained
without constant reliance on the old sectarian battle-cries and that
some greater effort should be made to win the co-operation of
the minority in efforts for the commmon good. Among Roman
catholics, there was more readiness than in the past to seek and
welcome opportunities for such co-operation. Though most of
them still held to the ideal of a united Ireland, there were many
who felt that it could not be attained in the foreseeable future, and
that they should therefore accept the existing situation and make
the best of it. On both sides, these more friendly attitudes were
encouraged by the contemporary spirit of ecumenism, which
affected Ireland, as it affected the rest of Christendom.

A change in the Northern Ireland government in 1963 marked
a critical stage in this development. The retiring prime minister,
Lord Brookeborough, had held office since 1941, and was regarded, perhaps rather unfairly, as an embodiment of the old-
fashioned unionism that had been hardened in the bitter struggle
of the early 1920s. His successor, Captain Terence O'Neill, was a
much younger man, more alert to present opportunities and
future developments than to fears inherited from the past. He
emphasised the need not only for a policy of reconciliation at
home but for the establishment of closer relations with the south,
and, in pursuance of this, he arranged an exchange of visits
with the prime minister of the republic. For a time, it seemed as
if a new era of peace and good-will was at hand.

But any attempt to change established patterns of political
behaviour is bound to be perilous. For forty years, unionist
leaders had appealed to the prejudices of protestants and had
done what they could to curtail the political influence of Roman

catholics; they could not now alter their course without arousing dangerous fears on one side and no less dangerous expectations on the other. The rank-and-file of the unionist party saw in O'Neill's policy a threat to their own monopoly of power; and the Roman catholics became more and more insistent that expressions of good-will should be translated into positive reforms, especially in the field of local government, which had hitherto been carefully organized so as to exclude them from effective control, even in areas where they formed a majority of the population. Almost suddenly, what had seemed a hopeful situation became one of bitter conflict. Fear on one side and impatience on the other frustrated the efforts of those who had hoped for the gradual development of mutual understanding and confidence.

From the beginning of O'Neill's premiership his attitude had caused alarm among some right-wing unionists, and this alarm had found a militant spokesman in Ian Paisley, a protestant preacher who had established a new sect calling itself the Free Presbyterian Church of Ulster. He appealed simultaneously to fears of a 'Romeward trend', which he claimed to detect in the older denominations, and to suspicions of a catholic conspiracy to drag Northern Ireland into the republic; and the popular response that he aroused in some quarters certainly influenced many M.P.s who were formally committed to supporting the prime minister's policy. On the other side, those who demanded immediate reforms organised themselves, after American example, in a Civil Rights movement, and conducted a series of marches and demonstrations. In the course of 1968 the two groups clashed more than once, both with each other and with the police; and a major riot in Londonderry in October inaugurated a prolonged period of civil disorder.

As violence spread, there was a significant change of tone. To begin with, the Civil Rights movement had had considerable protestant support, and it had concentrated on the need for certain specific reforms, in particular, an extension of the local government franchise. But it soon became in fact, though not in principle, a sectarian body; and its aims became both vaguer and more extensive. Many of its members, and many of the groups and organisations associated more or less closely with it, were not now likely to be satisfied by any reforms within the existing constitutional framework. They were in general agreement that unionism must be totally destroyed; and those among them who disclosed any constructive plans for the future favoured, for the most part, a workers' republic on the pattern put forward, more than half-a-century earlier, by James Connolly.

In face of this situation, right-wing influence in the unionist party grew stronger, and O'Neill's leadership came under heavy attack. In a general election, in February 1969, he tried to rally public opinion behind a programme of moderate reform; but the result did nothing to improve his position, and a few months later he was forced out of office, and succeeded by Major James Chichester-Clark, a former member of his cabinet. The change of leadership did not, however, mean a change of policy. By this time, indeed, a change of policy was virtually impossible. The government at Westminster, where Labour was in office, had become deeply concerned about the situation in Northern Ireland and had made it clear that the programme of reform announced by O'Neill must be speedily completed. Under the terms of the Government of Ireland Act, the Westminster parliament possessed the constitutional powers necessary to give effect to this decision; but, in practice, recourse to these powers was not likely to be necessary, for the economic and financial dependence of Northern Ireland on the rest of the United Kingdom was such that no government there could hope to function satisfactorily in defiance of the government in London. The fact that the conservative opposition at Westminster was equally insistent on the necessity for reforms in Northern Ireland made the isolation of the right-wing unionists complete.

The fall of O'Neill had been followed by several weeks of comparative tranquillity. But the extremists on both sides were preparing to renew the struggle; and in August fresh fighting broke out on a scale that the police could not hope to control. The British government now sanctioned the use of troops; the forces normally stationed in Northern Ireland were rapidly expanded; and with this help order was restored. But it was clear that the peace was precarious and that its maintenance would depend, for an indefinite period, on the continued use of the army.

The peace that the army had imposed was only partial, for the I.R.A. took advantage of the situation to resume its activities, basing itself, as in the 1920s, on the Roman catholic area of Belfast. Right-wing unionists demanded stronger measures of repression; and in face of their criticisms Chichester-Clark resigned early in 1971. But his successor, Brian Faulkner, refused to be hurried into rash decisions, and continued his predecessor's policy, though with a greater appearance of activity. His main purpose was to restore confidence, both within the unionist party and among the population as a whole, while leaving the security forces to contain and wear down the resistance of the I.R.A. It was a purpose that had the full support of both major parties in Great Britain, and one that even the government of the republic, alarmed at the probable repercussions of continued violence in the north, could hardly wish to see fail.

Thus things stood in 1971, fifty years after the signing of the treaty; and on the surface it might seem that the clock had been turned back and that all the old problems that partition had been designed to solve, or at least to alleviate, remained unchanged and unchangeable. Among right-wing unionists in the north there were those who felt that the critical days of 1912–14 had returned, and who were ready not only to fight the 'rebels' but to defy any British government whose policy threatened their own monopoly of power. Only the active presence of the crown forces prevented the outbreak of a civil war in which the whole of Ireland must become ruinously involved. But this superficial appearance belied the realities of the situation. Half-a-century of history could not be wiped out; and the political, economic and social changes of that period had created a new Ireland whose future, whatever it might be, would be shaped by their influence. Yet one thing stood fast: in 1971 as in 1921 it was clear that the real partition of Ireland was not on the map but in the minds of men.

READING LIST

The list of books given here is intended mainly for the general reader. The more serious student should consult, in the first place, E. M. Johnston, *Irish history: a select bibliography* (Historical Association, London, 1969). The following are useful for detailed treatment of particular periods: Conyers Read, *Bibliography of British history, Tudor period* (Oxford, 1933); Godfrey Davis, *Bibliography of British history, Stuart period* (Oxford, 1928); Pargellis and Medley, *Bibliography of British history: the 18th century, 1714–89* (Oxford, 1951). An annual list of 'Writings on Irish history' is published in *Irish historical studies* (Dublin, 1938–   ), beginning with a list for 1936. It should be noted that many works primarily concerned with British history, especially of the nineteenth and twentieth centuries, contain a great deal of matter relating to Ireland and Anglo-Irish relations; but these are not listed here.

The best general history is still Edmund Curtis, *History of Ireland* (6th ed., London, 1951). R. Dunlop, *Ireland from the earliest times to the present day* (Oxford, 1922) is much shorter, but stimulating. Brian Inglis, *The Story of Ireland* (2nd ed., London, 1966) is a lively introduction, with emphasis on the contemporary situation. T. W. Moody and F. X. Martin (ed.), *The course of Irish history* (Cork, 1967) is a co-operative work which combines authority with popular appeal, and is lavishly illustrated. Oliver MacDonagh, *Ireland* (Englewood Cliffs, New Jersey, 1968) is a penetrating commentary, with emphasis on the modern period. J. C. Beckett, *The making of modern Ireland,*

1603–1923 (London and New York, 1966) contains a useful critical bibliography.

For ecclesiastical history, there is no satisfactory general work. W. A. Phillips (ed.), *History of the Church of Ireland* (3 vols., Oxford, 1933–4), J. S. Reid, *History of the presbyterian church in Ireland* (ed. W. D. Killen, 3 vols., Belfast, 1867) and J. M. Barkley, *Short history of the presbyterian church in Ireland* (Belfast, 1959) are very useful within the limits indicated in their titles. A *History of Irish Catholicism* (ed. P. J. Corish) is in course of publication (Dublin, 1967–).

G. A. Hayes-McCoy, *Irish battles* (London, 1969) is, in fact, a history of warfare in Ireland, by the leading authority on the subject. L. M. Cullen, *Life in Ireland* (London, 1968) provides an outline of social history. E. Curtis and R. B. McDowell, *Irish historical documents, 1172–1922* (London, 1943) contains a selection of constitutional documents, with brief introductory notes. T. W. Freeman, *Ireland: its physical, historical, social and economic geography* (London, 1950) provides useful background information.

ANCIENT AND MEDIEVAL

ARMSTRONG, O., *Edward Bruce's invasion of Ireland* (London, 1923)
BIELER, Ludwig, *The life and legend of St Patrick* (Dublin, 1949)
BRYAN, D., *The great earl of Kildare* (Dublin, 1933)
CURTIS, E., *History of medieval Ireland* (2nd ed., London, 1938)
EVANS, E. E., *Prehistoric and early Christian Ireland* (London, 1966)
GWYNN, A., *The medieval province of Armagh* (Dundalk, 1946)
HUGHES, K., *The Church in early Irish society* (London, 1966)
MACALISTER, R. A. S., *Ancient Ireland* (London, 1935); *The archaeology of Ireland* (2nd ed., London, 1949)
MACNEILL, E., *Phases of Irish history* (Dublin, 1919); *Celtic Ireland* (Dublin, 1921)
O'DONOVAN, J. (trans.), *Annals of the Four Masters* (7 vols., Dublin, 1848–51)
O'RAHILLY, T. F., *The two Patricks* (Dublin, 1942); *Early Irish history and mythology* (Dublin, 1946)
ORPEN, G. H., *Ireland under the Normans* (4 vols., Oxford, 1911–20)
OTWAY-RUTHVEN, A. J., *A history of medieval Ireland* (London, 1968)
RAFTERY, J., *Prehistoric Ireland* (London, 1951)
RICHARDSON, H. G. and SAYLES, G. O., *The Irish parliament in the middles ages* (Philadelphia, 1952)

THE TUDOR CONQUEST

BAGWELL, R., *Ireland under the Tudors* (3 vols., London, 1885–90)
BUTLER, W. F. T., *Confiscation in Irish history* (2nd ed., Dublin, 1918)
EDWARDS, R. D., *Church and state in Tudor Ireland* (Dublin, 1935)
FALLS, C., *Elizabeth's Irish wars* (London, 1950)
HAYES-McCOY, G. A., *Scots mercenary forces in Ireland, 1565–1603* (Dublin, 1937)
LONGFIELD, A. K., *Anglo-Irish trade in the sixteenth century* (London, 1929)

MAXWELL, C., *Irish history from contemporary sources, 1509–1610* (London, 1929)

MORLEY, H. (ed.), *Ireland under Elizabeth and James I* (London, 1890) [Contains works relating to Ireland by Edmund Spenser, Sir John Davies and Fynes Moryson]

O'FAOLAIN, Sean, *The Great O'Neill* (London, 1942)

QUINN, D. B., *The Elizabethans and the Irish* (Cornell University Press, 1966)

RONAN, M., *The reformation in Dublin, 1534–1588* (London, 1926); *The reformation in Ireland under Elizabeth* (London, 1930)

WILSON, Philip, *The beginnings of modern Ireland* (London, 1921)

THE SEVENTEENTH CENTURY

BAGWELL, R., *Ireland under the Stuarts* (3 vols., London, 1909–16)

BURGHCLERE, Lady, *Life of James, first duke of Ormonde* (2 vols., London, 1912)

BUTLER, W. F. T., *Confiscation in Irish history* (2nd ed., Dublin, 1918)

CAMBLIN, G., *The town in Ulster* (Belfast, 1951)

CARTY, James, *Ireland from the flight of the earls to Grattan's parliament (1607–1782): a documentary record* (Dublin, 1949)

CLARKE, A., *The Old English in Ireland, 1625–42* (London, 1966)

COFFEY, D., *O'Neill and Ormond* (Dublin, 1941)

CULLEN, L. M., *Anglo-Irish trade, 1660–1800* (Manchester, 1968)

FALKINER, C. Litton, *Illustrations of Irish history and topography* (London, 1904)

KEARNEY, H., *Strafford in Ireland, 1633–41* (Manchester, 1959)

MACLYSAGHT, E., *Irish life in the seventeenth century* (2nd ed., Cork, 1950)

MOODY, T. W., *The Londonderry plantation, 1609–41* (Belfast, 1939)

MURRAY, A. E., *Commercial and financial relations between England and Ireland, from the period of the restoration* (London, 1903)

MURRAY, R. H., *Revolutionary Ireland and its settlement* (London, 1911)

O'BRIEN, G., *Economic history of Ireland in the seventeenth century* (Dublin, 1919)

O'BRIEN, R. B. (ed.), *Studies in Irish history 1603–49* (Dublin, 1906); *Studies in Irish history, 1649–1775* (2nd ed., Dublin, 1909)

PRENDERGAST, J. P., *The Cromwellian settlement* (2nd ed., London, 1870)

SEYMOUR, St John D., *The puritans in Ireland, 1647–61* (Oxford, 1921)

SIMMS, J. G., *The Treaty of Limerick,* (Dublin, 1961); *Jacobite Ireland, 1688-1691* (London, 1969)

THE PROTESTANT NATION

BECKETT, J. C., *Protestant dissent in Ireland, 1687–1780* (London, 1948)

BOLTON, G. C., *The passing of the Irish act of union* (Oxford, 1966)

BURKE, E., *Letters, speeches and tracts on Irish affairs* (ed. Matthew Arnold, London, 1881)

CARRÉ, Albert, *L'influence des Huguenots français en Irlande au xviie et xviiie siècles* (Paris, 1937)

CARTY, James, *Ireland from the flight of the earls to Gratton's parliament* (Dublin, 1949); *Ireland from Gratton's parliament to the great famine* (Dublin, 1949)

CONNELL, K. H., *The population of Ireland, 1750–1845* (Oxford, 1950)

CORKERY, D., *The hidden Ireland* (Dublin, 1925)

CRAIG, M. J., *Dublin, 1660–1860* (London, 1952); *The volunteer earl* (London, 1948) [The 'volunteer earl' is James Caulfeild, first earl of Charlemont]

CULLEN, L. M., *Anglo-Irish trade, 1660–1800* (Manchester, 1968)

DICKSON, R. J., *Ulster emigration to colonial America, 1718–1775* (London, 1966)

DUNLOP, R., *Henry Grattan* (London, 1889)

FALKINER, C. Litton, *Studies in Irish history and biography* (London, 1902)

FERGUSON, D., *Jonathan Swift and Ireland* (University of Illinois Press, 1962)

FROUDE, J. A., *The English in Ireland in the eighteenth century* (new ed., 3 vols., London, 1881)

GWYNN, S., *Henry Grattan and his Times* (London, 1939)

JACOB, R., *The rise of the United Irishmen* (London, 1937)

JOHNSTON, Edith M., *Great Britain and Ireland, 1760–1800* (Edinburgh, 1963)

LANDA, L. A., *Swift and the Church of Ireland* (Oxford, 1954)

LECKY, W. E. H., *History of Ireland in the eighteenth century* (new ed., 5 vols., London, 1892); *Leaders of public opinion in Ireland,* i (new ed., London, 1912) [Studies of Flood and Grattan]

LYNCH, P. and VAIZEY, J., *Guinness's Brewery in the Irish economy, 1759–1876* (Cambridge, 1960)

MCDOWELL, R. B., *Irish public opinion, 1750–1800* (London, 1944)

MCNEILL, M., *Mary Ann McCracken* (Dublin, 1960)

MAXWELL, C., *Dublin under the Georges* (London, 1936); *Country and town in Ireland under the Georges* (2nd ed., Dundalk, 1949)

MURRAY, A. E., *Commercial and financial relations between England and Ireland from the period of the restoration* (London, 1903)

O'BRIEN, G., *Economic history of Ireland in the eighteenth century* (Dublin, 1918)

O'BRIEN, R. B. (ed.), *Autobiography of Theobald Wolfe Tone* (2 vols., London, 1893); *Studies in Irish history, 1649–1775* (2nd ed., Dublin, 1909)

PAKENHAM, T., *The year of liberty: the great Irish rebellion of 1798* (London, 1969)

SIMMS, J. G., *The Williamite confiscation in Ireland, 1690–1703* (London, 1956)

SWIFT, J., *Drapier's letters* (ed. H. Davis, Oxford, 1935)

WALL, M., *The Penal Laws, 1691–1760* (Dublin, 1961)

YOUNG, Arthur, *Tour in Ireland, 1776–9* (ed. A. W. Hutton, London, 1962)

IRELAND UNDER THE UNION

AKENSON, D. H., *The Irish education experiment: the National system of Education in the nineteenth century* (London, 1970)

BLACK, R. D. C., *Economic thought and the Irish question, 1817–1870* (Cambridge, 1960)

BONN, M. J., *Modern Ireland and her agrarian problem* (trans. T. W. Rolleston, Dublin, 1906)

BROEKER, G., *Rural disorder and police reform in Ireland, 1812–36* (London, 1970)

CARTY, James, *Ireland from Grattan's parliament to the great famine* (Dublin, 1949); *Ireland from the great famine to the treaty* (Dublin, 1951)

CAULFIELD, M., *The Easter Rebellion* (London, 1964)

CHART, D. A., *Ireland from the union to catholic emancipation* (London, 1910)

CONNELL, K. H., *The population of Ireland, 1750–1845* (Oxford, 1950); *Irish peasant society* (Oxford, 1968)

CONROY, J. C., *History of railways in Ireland* (London, 1928)

CURTIS, L. P., Jr., *Coercion and conciliation in Ireland 1880–92* (Princeton, 1963)

DAVITT, M., *The fall of feudalism in Ireland* (London, 1904)

DIGBY, M., *Horace Plunkett, an Anglo-American Irishman* (Oxford, 1949)

DUFFY, C. Gavan, *League of north and south* (London, 1886)

DUNLOP, R., *Daniel O'Connell* (New York, 1906)

EDWARDS, R. D. and WILLIAMS, T. D. (ed.), *The great famine: studies in Irish history* (Dublin, 1956)

FREEMAN, T. W., *Pre-famine Ireland* (London, 1957)

GREEN, E. R. R., *The Lagan valley, 1800–1850. A local history of the industrial revolution* (London, 1949)

GWYNN, Denis, *The struggle for catholic emancipation* (London, 1928); *Young Ireland and 1848* (Cork, 1949)

HAMMOND, J. L., *Gladstone and the Irish Nation* (London, 1938)

HARKNESS, D., *The restless dominion: the Irish Free State and the British Common-wealth of Nations, 1921–31* (London, 1969)

HENRY, R. M., *The evolution of Sinn Fein* (Dublin, 1920)

HOLT, E., *Protest in arms: the story of the Irish troubles, 1916–1923* (London, 1960)

LECKY, W. E. H., *Leaders of public opinion in Ireland*, ii (new ed., London, 1912) [A study of Daniel O'Connell]

LYONS, F. S. L., *The Irish parliamentary party, 1890–1910* (London, 1951); *The fall of Parnell* (London, 1960); *John Dillon: a biography* (London, 1968); *Ireland since the famine* (London, 1971)

MACCAFFREY, James, *History of the catholic church in the nineteenth century* (2 vols., Dublin, 1909)

MACINTYRE, A., *The Liberator: Daniel O'Connell and the Irish party, 1830–1847* (London, 1965)

MCDOWELL, R. B., *Public opinion and government policy in Ireland, 1801–1846* (London, 1952); *The Irish administration, 1801–1914* (London, 1964); *The Irish Convention, 1917–18* (London, 1970)

MANSERGH, N., *Ireland in the age of reform and revolution* (London, 1940); revised and reissued as *The Irish question, 1840–1921* (London, 1965)

MARJORIBANKS, E. and COLVIN, I., *Life of Lord Carson* (2 vols., London, 1932, 1934)

MARTIN, F. X. (ed.), *Leaders and men of the Easter rising: Dublin, 1916* (London, 1967)

MOODY, T. W. (ed.), *The Fenian movement* (Cork, 1968)

MOODY, T. W. and BECKETT, J. C. (ed.), *Ulster since 1800* (1st and 2nd series, London, 1954, 1957)

NORMAN, E. R., *The Catholic church and Ireland in the age of revolution* (London, 1965)

NOWLAN, K. B., *The politics of Repeal: a study in the relations between Great*

O'BRIEN, Conor Cruise, *Parnell and his party, 1880–1890* (Oxford, 1957); (ed.), *The shaping of modern Ireland* (London, 1960)
Britain and Ireland, 1841–50 (London, 1965)

O'BRIEN, G., *Economic history of Ireland from the union to the famine* (London, 1921)

O'BRIEN, R. B., *Life and letters of Thomas Drummond* (London, 1889); *Life of Charles Stewart Parnell* (2 vols., London, 1898)

O'BRIEN, William and RYAN, Desmond (ed.), *Devoy's postbag, 1871–1928* (2 vols., Dublin, 1948, 1953) [Correspondence of a Fenian leader]

O'CONNOR, F., *The big fellow. A life of Michael Collins* (London, 1937)

O'CONNOR, Sir J., *History of Ireland, 1798–1924* (2 vols., London, 1925)

O'FAOLAIN, Sean, *King of the beggars* (London, 1938) [A biograply of Daniel O'Connell]

O'HEGARTY, P. S., *History of Ireland under the union* (London, 1952)

PAUL-DUBOIS, L., *Contemporary Ireland* (Dublin, 1908) [English translation of a work published in Paris in 1907]

PHILLIPS, W. A., *The revolution in Ireland, 1906–1923* (London, 1923)

POMFRET, J. E., *The struggle for the land in Ireland, 1800–1923* (Princeton, 1930)

RYAN, A. P., *Mutiny at the Curragh* (London, 1956)

SENIOR, H., *Orangeism in Ireland and Britain, 1795–1836* (London, 1966)

STEWART, A. T. Q., *The Ulster crisis* (London, 1967)

STRAUSS, E., *Irish nationalism and British democracy* (London, 1951)

THORNLEY, D., *Isaac Butt* (London, 1964)

WHITE, T. de V., *The Road of excess* (Dublin, 1946) [A biography of Isaac Butt]

WHYTE, J. H., *The independent Irish party, 1850–9* (Oxford, 1958)

WILLIAMS, D. (ed.), *The Irish struggle, 1916–1926* (London, 1966)

WOODHAM-SMITH, C., *The Great Hunger* (London, 1962)

IRELAND SINCE THE TREATY

HAND, G. J. (ed.), *Report of the Irish boundary commission, 1925* (Irish University Press, 1969)

LAWRENCE, R. J., *The Government of Northern Ireland* (Oxford, 1965)

LONGFORD, Earl of, and O'NEILL, T. P., *De Valera* (London, 1970)

LYONS, F. S. L., *Ireland since the famine* (London, 1971)

MACARDLE, D., *The Irish republic* (4th ed., Dublin, 1951)

MCCRACKEN, J. L., *Representative government in Ireland: Dáil Eireann, 1919-48* (Oxford, 1958)

MANSERGH, N., *The Irish Free State: its government and politics* (London, 1934); *The government of Northern Ireland: a study in devolution* (London, 1936)

NEILL, D. G., *Devolution of government, the experiment in Northern Ireland* (1953)

O'FAOLAIN, Sean, *De Valera* (London, 1939)

O'SULLIVAN, D., *The Irish Free State and its senate* (London, 1940)

PAKENHAM, F., *Peace by ordeal* (London, 1935) [Deals with the background and consequences of the settlement of 1921]

RYAN, D., *Unique dictator. A Study of Eamon de Valera* (London, 1936)

SHEARMAN, Hugh, *Not an inch: a study of Northern Ireland and Lord Craigavon* (London, 1943)

WHITE, T. de V., *Kevin O'Higgins* (London, 1948)

WILSON, T. (ed.), *Ulster under home rule* (Oxford, 1956)

INDEX

Butler, Thomas, 60
Butt, Isaac, 150–1

CAMPERDOWN, 126
Carlow (county), 34
Carlow (liberty), 23
Carrickfergus, 21, 22, 27, 75
Carson, Sir Edward (later Lord Carson of Duncairn), 156, 157, 158, 170
Casement, Sir Roger, 160
Cashel, 14, 16, 17
Castle chamber, court of, 56, 73
Castlereagh, Robert Stewart, Viscount (later 2nd marquis of Londonderry), 127
Catholic Association, 137–8
Catholic Emancipation, 128, 137–8
'Catholic rent', 138, 141
Cattle acts, 87, 109
Chamberlain, Neville, 175
Charlemont, James Caulfeild, 4th Viscount (later 1st earl of), 113 and n., 114, 118
Charles I, Irish policy of, 68, 70–1, 75, 78; 56, 64, 65, 66
Charles II, 80, 82, 83, 84–5, 86–7, 88, 89, 90, 94
Charles V, Holy Roman Emperor, 41
Chichester, Sir Arthur (later Baron Chichester of Belfast), 67
Chichester-Clark, James, 182
Church: before Anglo-Norman conquest, 12–13, 15–16, 17, 18; in later middle ages, 29, 46–7; in reformation period, 46–50, 58; under early Stuarts, 62–3, 65, 68, 71; in Restoration period, 85–6; at Revolution, 93; in 18th century, 101, 128, 129; under the union, 130, 135, 139, 149. See Papacy, Roman Catholics, Tithes.
Churchill, Lord Randolph, 155
Civil Rights Movement, 181–2
Civil War (1922–3), 168–9, 170
Clanricard, earldom of, 44, 46
Clare, 80
Clare, John Fitzgibbon, 1st earl of, 127 and n., 128
Clontarf, 14, 15, 142
Coercion acts, 131, 135, 147
Coleraine, 66
Collins, Michael, 165, 166, 168, 169, 172
Columba, St, 13

Commons, house of (English, British), 72, 88–9, 138, 156
Commons, house of (Irish): management of, 103, 113, 123; patriot opposition in, 103–4, 114, 117–18, 127–8; oratory of, 111; proposed reform of, 122; Connaught: O'Connor kingdom of, 18, 22, 26; Normans in, 19, 26, 27, 28, 29; royal authority in, 32, 33, 56; 'composition' of, 56; presidency of, 56; 15, 16, 24, 50, 59, 60, 61, 70, 80
Connolly, James, 157, 158–9, 182
Constitution of 1936, 175
Convocation, 71, 86, 101
Cooke, Henry, 142
Cork, 14, 68, 77, 143
Corn laws, repeal of, 144, 146–7
Cornwallis, Charles, 1st Marquis Cornwallis, 127
Cosgrave, William Thomas, 172, 173, 174
Costello, John Aloysius, 177
Courcy, John de, 19
Craigavon, James Ctaig, 1st Viscount, 156, 170
Cromer, George, 47
Cromwell, Oliver, 76, 79, 82
Cromwellian settlement, 80–2, 83–4, 86, 93
Cullen, Paul, 148

DAIL EIREANN, 161–2, 166, 168, 174, 175
Davitt, Michael, 151
Deputyship, 34 n.
Derry, 13, 15, See Londonderry.
De Valera, Eamon, 162, 165, 168, 172, 174–6, 177
Devlin, Joseph, 170
Donegal, 66
Dowdall, George, 48
Down, 12, 66, 76, 85, 126, 163
Drogheda, 33, 36, 63, 76, 79–80, 93
Drummond, Thomas, 140
Dublin Castle, 34, 42, 74, 130
Dublin (city): an invaders' capital, 9, 20; Norsemen in, 14, 15; commerce of, 24, 42, 63; importance in 18th century, 110–11, 120; insurrection in (1916), 159, 160–1; 18, 20, 21, 32, 33, 36, 39, 41, 48, 49, 56, 68, 75, 78, 79, 81, 82, 94, 103, 106, 114, 115, 117, 118, 122, 124, 130, 163, 170, 171

Index